Hopewell Junction:
A Railroader's Town

Hopewell Junction: A Railroader's Town

A History of Short-line Railroads in Dutchess County, New York

Bernard L. Rudberg
John M. Desmond

EXCELSIOR
EDITIONS

Cover photo taken by Ken Cochrane in July 1950 (at Hopewell Junction) from the Collection of J. W. Swanberg.

Published by State University of New York Press, Albany

© 2022 State University of New York

All rights reserved

Printed in the United States of America

No part of this book may be used or reproduced in any manner whatsoever without written permission. No part of this book may be stored in a retrieval system or transmitted in any form or by any means including electronic, electrostatic, magnetic tape, mechanical, photocopying, recording, or otherwise without the prior permission in writing of the publisher.

Excelsior Editions is an imprint of the State University of New York Press

For information, contact State University of New York Press, Albany, NY
www.sunypress.edu

Library of Congress Cataloging-in-Publication Data

Names: Rudberg, Bernard L., author. | Desmond, John Michael, author.
Title: Hopewell junction : a railroader's town : a history of short-line railroads in Dutchess County, New York / Bernard L. Rudberg, John M. Desmond.
Description: Albany : State University of New York Press, [2022] | Series: Excelsior editions | Includes bibliographical references and index.
Identifiers: LCCN 2022009664 | ISBN 9781438490700 (pbk. : alk. paper) | ISBN 9781438490694 (ebook)
Subjects: LCSH: Railroads—New York (State)—Dutchess County—History. | Railroad law—New York (State)—Dutchess County. | Dutchess County (N.Y.)—History.
Classification: LCC HE2771.N7 R83 2023 | DDC 385.09747/33—dc23/eng/20220404
LC record available at https://lccn.loc.gov/2022009664

10 9 8 7 6 5 4 3 2 1

*To those who envisioned and created the railroads
in Dutchess County, New York; who built and
operated the Dutchess County railroads; and who restored
and replicated the remains of these railroads*

Contents

List of Illustrations		ix
Introduction		1
Chapter 1	Before the Rails Reached Hopewell	5
Chapter 2	After the Rails Reached Hopewell	17
Chapter 3	Glimpses into the Standard Operating Procedures of a Short-Haul Railroad: The *Letter Books* of the ND&CRR	35
Chapter 4	Rivals of the Newburg, Dutchess, and Connecticut Railroad	53
Chapter 5	The Birth of Hopewell Junction	69
Chapter 6	Changes to Hopewell Junction	79
Chapter 7	Living in Hopewell Junction: 1920s–1950s	91
Chapter 8	Working the Rails: 1960–1974	103
Chapter 9	More Rails Depart Hopewell	117

| Chapter 10 | Restoring the Depot | 125 |

| Appendix | Recent Photographs of the Restored Depot, the Replicated Signal Station, and the Newly Constructed Bernard Rudberg Pavilion | 143 |

Works Cited   149

Index   153

Illustrations

Historic Railroad Lines in Dutchess County, New York. Courtesy of the Poughkeepsie Dutchess Transportation Council.   3

"Old" Hopewell Dutch Reformed Church. The Dutch Reformed Church in East Fishkill, New York, and the location of "Old" Hopewell, New York. The viewpoint is from what is now named the Beekman Road. The original post office of Hopewell was located across the street from the church on what is now named the Clove Branch Road.   22

"New" Hopewell Junction Post Office. The building is a residential home at 7 Railroad Avenue. Photograph Courtesy of the East Fishkill Historical Society.   23

Railroad Avenue, Hopewell Junction, New York. The viewpoint is east down Railroad Avenue. In the foreground on the right side of the frame sits the Hopewell Junction depot at its original location at the corner of Bridge Street and Railroad Avenue. The white building behind the depot is Borden's Creamery. On the left side of the frame is the Hopewell Inn, and two buildings down is the Hopewell Junction post office. Photograph from the Private Collection of Bernard L. and Celeste Rudberg, Courtesy of Celeste Rudberg.   24

Advertisement for the Newburgh, Dutchess, and Connecticut Railroad.   29

The *Washington* and Its Tender Crossing a Trestle. Photograph from the Private Collection of J. W. Swanberg, Courtesy of J. W. Swanberg. — 30

Engine #6 and Its Tender and Crew. Photograph from the Private Collection of J. W. Swanberg, Courtesy of J. W. Swanberg. — 33

Fishkill Landing. Photograph Courtesy of Beacon Historical Society. — 38

The Tioranda Bridge over the Fishkill Creek in Mattawan (Now Beacon), after 1876. — 44

The Ferry William Hart. Photograph Courtesy of Beacon Historical Society. — 47

Running through the Snow. Photograph from the Private Collection of J. W. Swanberg, Courtesy of J. W. Swanberg. — 50

Building the Poughkeepsie and Eastern Railroad. Photograph from the Private Collection of J. W. Swanberg, Courtesy of J. W. Swanberg. — 54

Poughkeepsie-Highland Bridge, c. 1904. Photograph by Detroit Publishing Co., Prints and Photograph Collection, Library of Congress. — 73

Announcement for the Dutchess County Railroad: "Ready for Business." — 75

Hopewell Junction Rail Yard. Photograph collection of the Late Ken Shuker. — 82

Hopewell Junction Depot, 1905. Photograph courtesy of the East Fishkill Historical Society. — 85

Relocated Hopewell Junction Depot. A photograph by J. P. Ahrens in April 1934 showing on the near left the Hopewell Junction Depot and on the far left the Hopewell Junction Freight House; in the middle, the double tracks of the New York, New Haven, and Hartford Railroad leading north to Poughkeepsie; and on right Signal Tower #196. Between the Depot and the Freight House is the single track of the old Newburgh, Dutchess, and Columbia Railroad running from Dutchess Junction to Millerton. Photograph from the Collection of J. W. Swanberg, Courtesy of J. W. Swanberg. 88

The Abandoned Track of the Newburgh, Dutchess, and Connecticut Railroad. In the center of the frame is the abandoned track, and beyond it, the empty roadbed of the Newburgh, Dutchess, and Connecticut Railroad (ND&CRR). The track was pulled up from Hopewell Junction to Millerton by 1938. To the left of the frame in the middle distance is the Hopewell Junction Freight House and to the right of the frame and in the middle distance is the Hopewell Junction Depot. Beyond the depot is Signal Station #196 soon to be torn down. Photograph from the Collection of J. W. Swanberg, Courtesy of J. W. Swanberg. 89

Rail Bus and Rail Bus with Two Drivers. Photographs from the Collection of J. W. Swanberg, Courtesy of J. W. Swanberg. 90

Charlotte Dodge's Saunter around Hopewell Junction, 1923. 92

Woman and Children in Hopewell Junction Rail Yard. What is unique about this rail-yard image is that in the foreground and to the right a woman and a girl walk along a side walk between sets of tracks, and in the middle ground and center three boys sit on a pile of railroad ties. Usually, photos only show male workers on and around the tracks. Photograph from the Collection of J. W. Swanberg, Courtesy of J. W. Swanberg. 93

Two Types of Locomotives Working at Hopewell Junction. Photograph by Kent Cochrane in July 1950 from the Collection of J. W. Swanberg, Courtesy of J. W. Swanberg. 104

The Hopewell Junction Depot Shortly after the Fire. A photograph by Austen McEntee of the Hopewell Junction Depot in 1986 shortly after the fire and before Metro-North boarded

Illustrations | xi

up the depot. The depot remained in this squalid condition until Rich Taylor discovered the almost unrecognizable building in 1994. Photograph from the Collection of J. W. Swanberg, Courtesy of J. W. Swanberg.   123

The Dilapidated Hopewell Junction Depot in 1994. Photograph by Richard Taylor from the Collection of Richard and Maureen Taylor, Courtesy of Richard and Maureen Taylor.   126

North Side of the Restored Hopewell Junction Depot Museum. Photograph by Richard Taylor from the Collection of Richard and Maureen Taylor, Courtesy of Richard and Maureen Taylor.   143

East Side of the Restored Hopewell Junction Depot Museum. Photograph by Richard Taylor from the Collection of Richard and Maureen Taylor, Courtesy of Richard and Maureen Taylor.   144

South Side of the Restored Hopewell Junction Depot Museum. Photograph by Richard Taylor from the Collection of Richard and Maureen Taylor, Courtesy of Richard and Maureen Taylor.   144

West Side of the Hopewell Junction Depot Museum. Photograph by Richard Taylor from the Collection of Richard and Maureen Taylor, Courtesy of Richard and Maureen Taylor.   145

West Waiting Room of the Hopewell Junction Depot Museum. Photograph by Richard Taylor from the Collection of Richard and Maureen Taylor, Courtesy of Richard and Maureen Taylor.   145

Station Agent's Office of the Hopewell Junction Depot Museum. Photograph by Richard Taylor from the Collection of Richard and Maureen Taylor, Courtesy of Richard and Maureen Taylor.   146

Telegrapher's Office of the Hopewell Junction Depot Museum. Photograph by Richard Taylor from the Collection of Richard and Maureen Taylor, Courtesy of Richard and Maureen Taylor.   146

East Waiting Room of the Hopewell Junction Depot Museum. Photograph by Richard Taylor from the Collection of Richard and Maureen Taylor, Courtesy of Richard and Maureen Taylor.   147

West Side of the Replica of Signal Station #196. Photograph by Richard Taylor from the Collection of Richard and Maureen Taylor, Courtesy of Richard and Maureen Taylor. 147

South Side of the Replica of Signal Station #196. Photograph by Richard Taylor from the Collection of Richard and Maureen Taylor, Courtesy of Richard and Maureen Taylor. 148

Bernard Rudberg Pavilion, Hopewell Junction Depot Museum. Photograph by Richard Taylor from the Collection of Richard and Maureen Taylor, Courtesy of Richard and Maureen Taylor. 148

Acknowledgments

Hopewell Junction: A Railroader's Town is a consolidation and expansion of the three books written by the late Bernard L. Rudberg about the history of the east-west, short-haul railroads that ran throughout Dutchess County, New York. These books are titled *Hopewell Junction: A Railroader's Town; Twenty-Five Years on the ND&C: A History of the Newburgh, Dutchess, and Connecticut Railroad;* and *Hopewell Depot: Railroad Years and Restoration 1873–2013.*

I am obliged to Mr. Wray Rominger, former publisher of Purple Mountain Press, Ltd., for suggesting to me that I consolidate Mr. Rudberg's three books to make a single history of the Hopewell Junction Depot, of the railroads that ran by it, and of the hamlet that grew up around it. I thank Ms. Celeste Rudberg, widow of Mr. Rudberg, who gave me permission to undertake this project, as well as the support of the 2020–22 Board of Trustees of the Hopewell Junction Depot Museum. I am indebted to Mr. Richard Carlin, senior acquisitions editor, the humanities, SUNY Press, for accepting my proposal to publish this work.

Of course, I am grateful to Bernard L. Rudberg himself for restoring and publishing the rich rail history not only of Hopewell Junction but also of Dutchess County. Once, I briefly met Mr. Rudberg when I was a curious, first-time visitor to the Hopewell Junction Depot. Now, I meet him often and for lengthy periods in the pages of his books.

Unquestionably, I am obliged, grateful, appreciative, and indebted to my wife, Karen.

Introduction

Hopewell Junction: A Railroader's Town narrates a history of the east-west, short-line railroads that ran throughout Dutchess County, New York, from 1869 to 1984. The narration centers on the connection of many of these short lines, the hamlet of Hopewell Junction in the town of East Fishkill, within Dutchess County; on the train depot built there by the Dutchess and Columbia Railroad circa 1873; and on the hamlet that grew up around the depot from circa 1873 to 1963.

The narrative focuses on four interrelated topics. The first topic is the rise, prosperity, and fall of the railroads that ran in Dutchess County and especially through Hopewell Junction. The second topic is the flourishing of the Hopewell Junction depot from circa 1873 to 1933, its gradual decline in importance, and its abandonment in 1986 by the last railroad to own it. The third topic is the appearance, growth, and departure of the hamlet surrounding the depot starting in about 1873 and ending in 1963 with the building of the large International Business Machine plant southwest of Hopewell Junction. The fourth topic is the successful restoration of the depot from 1996 to 2021 as a designated museum of the Education Department of the State of New York and as a historic and architectural resource on the New York State Register of Historical Places by the New York State Historic Preservation Office and on the National Register of Historic Places by the National Park Service.

In general, *Hopewell Junction: A Railroader's Town* informs the reader who may not be aware of the abandoned bridge abutments and rutted rail beds hidden in the trees and tucked away in private backyards of the extent of the east-west, short-line railroads that crisscrossed Dutchess County and ran through Hopewell Junction. The book explains the transforming albeit relatively brief presence of these railroads on the rural countryside and on the agricultural and small-mill communities of Dutchess County, including Hopewell Junction, during the last half of the nineteenth and most of the twentieth centuries. It chronicles the destruction and abandonment by the failing railroads of their unproductive assets, such as the rails that ran past the Hopewell Junction depot and the building itself. It illustrates the arrival and departure of Hopewell Junction as the hamlet surrounding the depot and the center of a railroad hub until that hub was terminated and the IBM plant was built. It recounts the resolve of volunteers in the last decade of the twentieth and first decades of the twenty-first century to reverse that abandonment by restoring and repurposing not only the few remaining assets of the failed and often forgotten railroads but also preserving the history and artifacts of these railroads and the railroader towns they created.

Railroad Names and Their Abbreviations

The following lists the railroad lines and their abbreviations mentioned in the book.

> Boston, Hartford, and Erie Railroad (BH&ERR)
> Central New England and Western Railroad (CNE&WRR)
> Central New England Railroad (CNERR)
> Clove Branch Railroad (CBRR)
> Connecticut and Western Railroad (C&WRR)
> Conrail Railroad (Conrail)
> Dutchess and Columbia Railroad (D&CRR)
> Dutchess County Railroad (DCRR)
> Dutchess County Railroad Company (DCRRC)
> East Tennessee and Virginia Railroad (ET&VRR)
> Erie Railroad (ERR)*
> Freehold & NY (F&NY) Railroad
> Hampshire and Hamden Railroad (H&HRR)
> Hartford and Connecticut Western Railroad (H&CWRR)

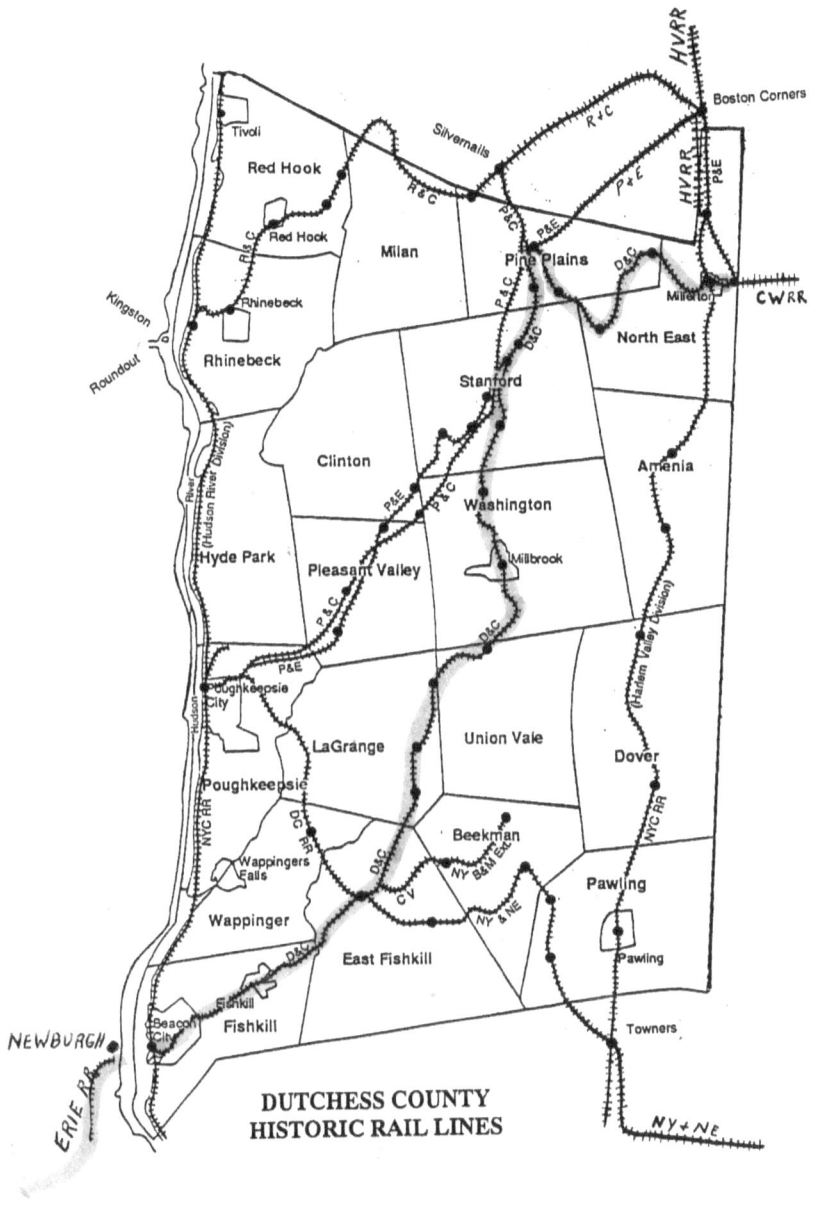

Historic Railroad Lines in Dutchess County, New York. Courtesy of the Poughkeepsie Dutchess Transportation Council.

Hartford, Providence, and Fishkill Railroad (HP&FRR)
Housatonic Railroad (HRR)
Hudson River Railroad (HRRR)*
Metro-North Railroad (MNR or Metro-North)
New England Railroad (NERR)
New York and Harlem Railroad (NY&HRR)*
New York and Massachusetts Railroad (NY&MRR)
New York and New England Railroad (NY&NERR)
New York Central Railroad (NYCRR)
New York City and Hudson River Railroad (NYC&HRRR)
New York, Boston, and Montreal Railroad (NYB&MRR)
New York, New Haven, and Hartford Railroad (NYNH&HRR)
Newburgh, Dutchess, and Connecticut Railroad (ND&CRR)
Penn Central Railroad (PCRR)
Pennsylvania Railroad (PRR)
Philadelphia and Reading Railroad (P&RRR)
Philadelphia, Reading, and New England Railroad Company (PR&NERRC)
Poughkeepsie and Connecticut Railroad (P&CRR)
Poughkeepsie and Eastern Railroad (P&ERR)
Poughkeepsie and Eastern Railroad Company (P&ERRC)
Poughkeepsie and South Eastern Railroad (P&SERR)
Poughkeepsie, Hartford, and Boston Railroad (PH&BRR)
Rhinebeck and Connecticut Railroad (R&CRR)

Chapter 1

Before the Rails Reached Hopewell

Why build a railroad in the nineteenth century? In "Promoting the Hudson River Railroad," Steven Lubar observes that

> cities and towns throughout the United States looked to railroads to bring them prosperity. Engineers and capitalists both partook of the railroad enthusiasm, aiming to profit not only from building lines but also from the economic development they trusted would follow. Yet decisions [. . .] were influenced [. . .] also by cultural, social, and psychological factors: [t]he perceived import of commerce, the relationship of urban areas to their hinterlands, beliefs about progress, faith in novel technologies. (55)

How, then, build a railroad whether in the nineteenth century or today? In *The Great Railroad Revolution*, Christian Wolmar highlights

> several elements [necessary] to come together: the technology, both for the traction and the track; the financing to pay for it; the permission of the state to build it; the creation of the appropriate legal framework; and, of course, the labor for construction.
> Such a coordination of different agencies, technologies, and resources [. . .] required vision and ambition, as well as

the cooperation of the various entities involved. It is hardly surprising, therefore, that the emergence of the railroads was a stuttering process, conducted in fits and starts with numerous failures and dead ends (2).

Railroad Failures

The state of New York issued a charter in 1832 to the Dutchess County Railroad Company (DCRR) to build a railroad from Poughkeepsie to the Connecticut state line. The new company conducted a survey of the rail route in 1833 but accomplished nothing else (Smith 97). The DCRR had the vision and ambition to imagine a railroad, the permission of the state to build a railroad, the appropriate legal framework to form a railroad company, and the fixed capital to finance a railroad. However, it did not acquire the technology and employ the labor (beyond the surveyors) to construct a railroad.

In anticipation of railroads not yet built and of profit not yet made, the Poughkeepsie Locomotive Engine Company was founded in 1838. The company built a factory in Poughkeepsie on the east bank of the Hudson River (Harlow 139–40); the site is below where the Mid-Hudson Children's Museum is located today. The company announced it would build seventy-five to one hundred locomotives per year. However, it only built one locomotive before going bankrupt in 1839 during a financial panic (Harlow 139–40).

The idea of an east-west railroad through Dutchess County did not always come from engineers and capitalists residing within the county. In 1849, the Connecticut General Assembly issued a charter to the Hartford, Providence, and Fishkill Railroad (HP&FRR). This company planned to join rails from Providence, Rhode Island, west to Hartford, Connecticut, then southwest through Dutchess County to Fishkill Landing (now Beacon), New York, and terminate at the Hudson River. The HP&FRR intended to establish a ferry service to carry the railroad cars directly across the Hudson to Newburgh, New York. In Newburgh, the cars would be coupled to an Erie Railroad (ERR) train. The ERR completed its first Newburgh

Branch in January 1850 (McCue 9). However, the HP&FRR never made it to Dutchess County. It went bankrupt in January 1858 (Mc Dermott 11).

> During this time of railroad failures in Dutchess County, "[t]he resident of the typical turnpike town lived among two or three thousand people in a few square miles that were surrounded by wilderness. Each town was a pocket of human association that seldom interacted with other towns, and then primarily for trade purposes. [. . .] They would see each other at church, at town meetings, and at the meetings of various volunteer societies." (Klein and Fielding 12)

For short distance "trade purposes," as well as land worth, turnpikes were vital. Yet, "[t]he turnpikes could not, crucially, tap into the most significant market, the long-distance transportation of [produce] such as wheat, corn, or pork because the tolls were simply too high [for the farmers transporting the produce] in relation to the value of the produce" (Wolmar 12). Farmers and manufacturers chose to transport their produce and goods to Albany and New York City by steamboat, sloop, and barge sailing on the Hudson River. Travelers followed suit with the farmers and manufacturers.

Railroad Success: The New York and Harlem Railroad

The New York and Harlem Railroad (NY&HRR) spiked down the first tracks in Dutchess County. The earliest train to cross the Dutchess County line arrived in Dover on New Year's Eve 1848 (*The Journal and Poughkeepsie Eagle*). The *Eagle* cites the optimistic prediction of the *New York Commercial Advertiser* on the event: "Thus the city [sic] of New York has effectually tapped the rich county of Dutchess, and the Harlem railroad will henceforth stand among the most successful and prosperous establishments of the country" (*The Journal and Poughkeepsie Eagle*).

The State of New York chartered the NY&HRR in 1831. Twenty-one years later, in 1852, the NY&HRR trains originated in Manhattan; continued north from Dover through Amenia and Millerton in Dutchess County and Chatham in Columbia County; connected with the Albany and West Stockbridge Railroad; and terminated in Albany, New York.

The NY&HRR benefited existing farms in the Harlem Valley region of Dutchess County by transporting their produce to Albany and New York City. The railroad also brought new and novel jobs to the county. Laborers, skilled and unskilled, lay down the rails, maintained the track, and built up freight and passenger stations. Clerks staffed the train stations as telegraphers and freight and passenger agents. Engineers, firemen, conductors, and brakemen operated the trains (Mc Dermott 14). Laborers tended to be young, single men who often followed the laying down of the rails as it progressed north to Albany. Clerks, on the other hand, tended to be older, family men who settled in the counties in which they worked (Mc Dermott 14).

E. Clarence Hyatt's *History of the New York and Harlem Railroad* refers to "an interesting article headed 'Reminiscences of Other Days' and signed 'A Veteran' [that] was published in a newspaper at Chatham in 1888." This article offers a view of the living conditions for the laborers laying NY&HRR track:

> The inhabitants of the primitive and rural section between Dover Plains and Chatham were astonished to see many boarding houses (shanties) built of hemlock wood put up along the line of road, indicated by little, square, numbered stakes driven into the ground. These shanties accommodated from 25 to 50 Irish laborers, who used to work for 75 cents a day and their board. They used to sleep in bunks around the side of the room, and sometimes the shanty had a floor, but oftener the carpet was mother earth. On the completion of the road in February 1852, so the passenger and freight trains could begin to run, many of the people along the line looked at a locomotive for the first time, for they had never ridden a foot on the rails [. . .]. (17)

The initial success of the NY&HRR, from 1852 to the mid-1850s, was followed by a period of decline. In *Iron Empires*, Michael Hiltzik explains this decline in many railroads as "[t]he line [falling] victim to the common ailments of American railroads of the era—looting by dishonest and incompetent executives, a lack of operating credit, physical decrepitude" (15–16). Cornelius Vanderbilt, who had invested in the NY&HRR, watched it decline. Then in 1862–63, he bought more stock, began to administer the railroad himself, and revived it (Hiltzik 16).

Railroad Success: The Hudson River Railroad

Meanwhile, on December 31, 1849, a year to the day after the New York and Harlem Railroad came into Dutchess County, the Hudson River Railroad (HRRR) reached Poughkeepsie (*The Journal and Poughkeepsie Eagle*). The *Eagle* editorialized, again optimistically, that "[c]ars have been running regularly, twice a day, between this place and New York. Henceforth an uninterrupted railroad communication will be kept up."

The State of New York chartered the HRRR in 1846. For the next three years, it had been a difficult line to build. For example, "[t]he bore through the nose of Breakneck Hill [. . .] gave endless trouble. The rock was so hard a workman hand-drilling all day (usually twelve hours) could punch only twelve to twenty-four inches into it" (Harlow 145–46).

That drilling detail suggests the folklore hero and possible historic figure John Henry. Henry, whether in fact or fiction, was employed in hammering a drill made of steel into solid rock to bore holes in the rock. Explosives were stuffed in the holes, were ignited, blasted the rock apart, and prepared a tunnel through which a railroad was built. A Black man, Henry purportedly engaged in a race with a drilling machine; he won the contest but died of exhaustion. He remains today as an icon of the railroad laborer's physical strength, superiority over machines, and racial self-respect.

When the laborers were not breaking through rock, they built bridges across bays, creek mouths, and estuaries. They constructed drawbridges for landowners along the waterways to sail into and out of the Hudson River. They filled the land up to the low-water mark and erected retaining walls to maintain the fill (Harlow 145–46).

When the line was completed from Poughkeepsie to Albany, it competed successfully with steamboat, sloop, and barge transportation both in travel time and winter travel. When the river froze, the steamboats, sloops, and barges often sat idle, and the railroad alone carried freight and passengers.

Like the NY&HRR, the HRRR benefitted Dutchess County businesses and farms. The railroad transported their goods and produce to Albany and New York City markets in larger bulks, by faster times, and during all seasons than could the steamboats, sloops, and barges. The two railroads transported travelers to New York City and Albany faster and in all seasons, too (Mc Dermott 18).

In the words of Lubar, the success of the two long-haul, north-south railroads authenticated "the importance of commerce, the relationship of urban areas to the hinterlands, the beliefs in progress, and the faith in novel technologies" (55).

An eyewitness to the successful construction of the HRRR in Fishkill Landing (now Beacon), James F. Brown, a gardener on the Verplanck family estate, Mount Guilian, noted in his 1849 diary that "[t]here was a very heavy blast from the rail roade [sic] [. . .] this afternoon about 5 o'clock which threw a number of stones near the garden fence, a distance of 40 rods [660 feet] (Brown).

On December 20, 1850, Brown mentions in his diary that he rode the train from New York City to Fishkill Landing. Brown was a freed Black. He does not remark on how he was treated by ticket agents and conductors. However, Frederick Douglas and Harriet Jacobs, who both escaped slavery and became leading abolitionists, remark on how they were treated while riding trains in the north before the Civil War. In *My Bondage and My Freedom*, Douglass observes:

> The custom of providing separate cars for the accommodation of colored travelers was established on nearly all the railroads of New England [. . .]. Regarding this custom as fostering the spirit of caste, I made it a rule to seat myself in the cars for the accommodation of passengers generally. Thus seated, I was sure to be called upon to betake myself to the "Jim Crow car." Refusing to obey, I was often dragged out of my seat, beaten, and severely bruised, by conductors and brakemen. (404)

Harriet Jacobs, in her autobiography *Incidents in the Life of a Slave Girl*, recounts an unpleasant occasion in which she was denied a ride in first class on a train from Philadelphia to New York City:

> When Mr. Durham handed us our tickets, he said, "I am afraid you will have a disagreeable ride, but I could not procure tickets for the first-class cars." Supposing I had not given him money enough, I offered more. "Oh, no," said he, "they could not be had for any money. They don't allow colored people to go in the first-class cars." This was the first chill to my enthusiasm about the Free States. [. . .] It made me sad to find how the north aped the customs of the south. (247)

After Appomattox:
The State of the Economy in Dutchess County

Between the NY&HRR and the HRRR, the goods and produce of the county were transported to markets beyond the county itself, namely, to New York City and Albany. In April 1865, the HRRR connected Dutchess County with a momentous current event beyond these two cities' limits. On April 15, President Abraham Lincoln died of gunshot wounds in the Petersen House across the street from Ford's Theater in Washington DC. Ten days later, on April 25, the funeral train carrying Abraham Lincoln's body and the "exhumed remains of his son Willie who died in 1862 at age 11" passed through Dutchess County on its way north to Albany then west to Springfield, Illinois (Ferro).

At the Dutchess Junction Station (a few miles south of the current Beacon Metro-North station), "In God We Trust" was spelled out in evergreen sprigs. People from Dutchess County as well as from Newburgh and New Paltz, cities across the Hudson River, lined both sides of the tracks as the train rolled slowly by at between two and five miles per hour (Ferro). At Poughkeepsie, the train stopped for fifteen minutes. Matthew Vassar, owner of the brewery and a founder of the college named for him, clipped magnolia blossoms from his tree, which still stands. Along with ladies holding other flowers, he went aboard the funeral car and placed them on the president's coffin (Ferro). The train left Poughkeepsie and steamed up to and through Rhinecliff, New York. People from Kingston watched from across the Hudson River for the belching smoke from the engine as a sign of the president's passing. Hence, the railroad connected Dutchess County not only with "nearby" Albany and New York City but also with "far away" Washington DC—and national history.

After the train passed, the mourners left the tracks and went home or to work. They worked along docks, in factories, on farms, at mills, and inside mines and quarries. They loaded and unloaded freight from barges, sloops, and steamships sailing from or to New York City and Albany. They brewed beer, baked bricks, created carpets, made machinery, and sewed hats. They grew grains and tended cows, horses, and pigs. They ground grain and sawed lumber. They bottled sparkling wines. They dug and hauled granite and iron ore.

Transporting goods and produce to one of the two north-south, long-haul railroads and/or to the river took time, especially from the factories, farms, mills, mines, and wineries located in the middle of the county. Traveling in horse- and mule-drawn wagons over dirt and gravel roads to the depots and docks was demanding. In winter, the roads were often piled with snow, so travel by wagon, horse, foot, and even sleigh was regularly impossible. In spring, snow melt and in fall incessant rain sopped the roads; churned them into mud; and bogged down wagon wheels, horses' hooves, and even booted feet. In drier summer, ruts rocked wagons and broke axels, broke horses' legs, and tripped walkers.

What would speed up this transportation was an interior railroad—or railroads—running east-west rather than north-south with several stations located in hamlets, towns, and villages throughout the middle of the county. If these railroads were built, the wagons would need to travel only short, albeit rough distances to the stations of these interior railroads. There the teamsters would unload their goods and produce into the freight cars. People, too, would travel only short distances to board a train. The interior railroads would connect with the north-south railroads or with the Hudson River steamships, sloops, and barges and thus with Albany and New York City. According to John Majewski and others:

To help themselves out of the mud, New Yorkers built thousands of miles of branch and spur railroads after the Civil War. [. . .] Small towns saw the railroads as the key to future prosperity. [. . .] [B]ranch railroads helped New Yorkers overcome poor roads by shortening the trip to the nearest train station. (27–28)

However, building the east-west, short-haul railroads in Dutchess County needed a more compelling reason than just the transportation of goods, produce, and people from Dutchess County to New York City and Albany. That motivation was the transportation of anthracite coal from northeast Pennsylvania to southern New England.

The Pennsylvania Coal Rush: Mining Anthracite Coal

Between 1820 and 1850, there occurred a gradual conversion in the way homeowners heated their houses and factory owners heated their buildings and powered their machines. While wood had been the preferred fuel in the past, it was being phased out in favor of coal. The preferred type of coal was anthracite, mined in northeastern Pennsylvania (Powell 12). The anthracite coal fields were—and are—located in Carbon, Lackawanna, Luzerne, and Schuylkill Counties in northeastern Pennsylvania. Anthracite coal was first mined in 1769, and by the 1820s, it was being mined in large quantities. In 1850, three million tons were excavated, which went to customers in other parts of Pennsylvania, New Jersey, and New York (Powell 12–13).

Anthracite is a hard, compact variety of coal. It has high carbon content, few impurities, and high energy density. It can be easily and quickly identified by its bright sheen. In one's hand, it feels hard and brittle yet clean to the touch. These characteristics differentiate it from bituminous coal. Although it is difficult to ignite, it admits a pale, blue flame when ignited, needs little attention to sustain its combustion, releases relatively little smoke, and leaves behind modest amounts of dust (Di Gianfrancesco 4). Thus, it became the coal of choice for factory owners and homeowners.

Transporting the tons of anthracite coal was a daunting project in 1850. Once the anthracite was above ground, it was loaded onto gravity railroad cars, which carried the coal down the mountains to flatter land. The mined anthracite and the miners themselves were kept fairly safe from excessive speed and possible derailment by the brakes on the cars. Once at the bottom of the incline, the anthracite was unloaded from the coal cars and loaded onto barges floating in inland canals and transported along a canal or a network of rivers and canals to cities and towns (Powell 13). The cars of the gravity railroad were attached to a wench powered by a steam engine and hauled back up the mountain.

One water route took the anthracite coal from Honesdale, Pennsylvania, on the Lackawaxen River to the Delaware River; on the Delaware River to Port Jervis, New York; and on the Delaware and Hudson Canal to the canal's Hudson River terminus at Kingston, New York. Mules pulled the barges along the 108-mile canal, tended first by children and later by men who walked between fifteen and twenty miles a day (Osterberg 72). At Kingston, the anthracite was unloaded from the canal barges and loaded onto steamboats, river barges, and sloops for points north and south along the river.

An article in the August 18, 1889, edition of the *New York Times* explains in part where the lodes of anthracite coal went after being transported along the Delaware and Hudson Canal to Kingston, New York:

> From the mouth of the Rondout Creek, which forms the harbor of the thriving and busy city of Kingston, can be seen emerging every evening huge rafts of canal boats, tall-mastered down-Easters, and barges of various sorts laden with cargoes [. . .] from the coal regions about Honesdale and Scranton, in Pennsylvania, all bound for this port and consigned to, perhaps, as many different persons as there are boats in the tow.

Before all the anthracite coal arrived in the port of New York City, several tons were detoured to the ports in Dutchess County: Dutchess Junction, Fishkill Landing, Poughkeepsie, and Rhinecliff. From these docks, it was loaded into the coal cars of the east-west, short-haul, railroads, transported across the county, and eventually into Massachusetts, Connecticut, and Rhode Island.

The Arrival of the Newburgh Branch of the Erie Railroad

Several canals were indispensable to the transportation of anthracite coal, including the Delaware and Hudson. However, in *Erie Railroad's Newburgh Branch*, Robert McCue observes:

> Canal boats moved at an average of four miles an hour, pulled along by mules. The advantage was not in speed but in tonnage The coming of the railroads, however, set speed records that no canal could come even close to matching, which brought the age of canals to a close. (8)

A railroad pacesetter was the Erie Railroad (ERR). It constructed a branch line from its main line in Orange County at Greycourt, near Chester, to Newburgh and opened it in January 1850. Because anthracite coal was a main cargo carried by the ERR in general and its Newburgh branch specifically, the Penn Coal Company built wharves on the Newburgh waterfront in 1867. The ERR constructed a second, somewhat shorter branch line from its main line at Harriman to Vales Gate on the older Newburgh branch line and opened it in July 1869 (McCue 8–9).

In the newspaper article "Giant Social Gathering of 1850," Mary Tamaney describes the first appearance of a train in Newburgh in January:

> At 1 p.m., as the first train whistle sounded down the Quassaick valley around the bend of the new rail line, a cannon was ready to return the salute with a load roar. Newburgh was poised for the wondrous event of seeing the first locomotive enter the village. [. . .] People cheered and watched the dignitaries give their speeches of celebration. Then the railroad owners and investors retired to the old United States Hotel for a dinner. They didn't ignore their audience, however. In the new "roundhouse" (a semi-circular brick stable for locomotives)

down on the riverfront, the Erie Railroad owners had laid out a feast for the public to enjoy for the rest of the day.

Travelers today along River Road in Newburgh pass under a bridge that supports the remaining track of the Newburgh Branch running approximately five miles from Vail's Gate to the Newburgh riverfront (McCue interview).

Twenty-five years before the arrival of the Newburgh Branch of the Erie Railroad, Newburgh had been an important commercial center on the Hudson River between New York City and Albany. It was the intersection of several roads leading to New Jersey, New York State, and Pennsylvania. It also was a port with several docks serving steamboats, sloops, and barges sailing up and down the river (Mott 42). But when the Erie Canal was finished and the Delaware and Hudson Canal was built, Newburgh declined as a commercial center. Realizing its weakened commercial state, Newburgh entrepreneurs and residents determined in 1830 "[t]o regain the prestige [their city] had lost, and to help it to a new and greater business eminence, [by deciding] that there could be no better means than the connecting of [the city] with the Pennsylvania coal fields by a railroad" (Mott 43). Thus, the cheerful celebration twenty years later, in 1850, when the Newburgh Branch eventually completed that connection to the coal fields. Nineteen years later, in 1869, it also completed the connection between the Pennsylvania coal fields and Dutchess County.

Newburgh lies directly across the Hudson River from southern Dutchess County. The coal piled in the Erie Railroad cars and on the Penn Coal Company docks was ferried across the Hudson to the docks at Dutchess Junction. There it was piled into the cars of the first east-west, short-haul railroad in Dutchess County, the Dutchess and Columbia Railroad (D&CRR).

Chapter 2

After the Rails Reached Hopewell

A Railroad of George Brown, by George Brown, and for George Brown: The Dutchess and Columbia Railroad

The central figure in founding, funding, building, and operating the D&CRR was George Hunter Brown. A native of New York City and a resident of the town of Washington, Brown became involved in the political affairs of both the town and Dutchess County and served as the town's supervisor in 1866. At that time, he also became involved in the D&CRR.

William Mc Dermott's explanation of how it was to be funded provides insight into the specific politics of building this first local, rural, east-west, short-haul railroad in Dutchess County:

> [Chairman] George Brown made clear he did, "not want capitalists from a distance to take stock in this road and so get control of it [. . .] as it was intended the road should belong to the poor people, and not to a few moneyed people." Yet, in only a slightly veiled threat, he reminded farmers along the route that if they and their town governments failed to invest, Brown would have to accept offers from Poughkeepsie investors. Then the line would be built from Poughkeepsie to Millerton by way of Pleasant Valley, Salt Point, Stanfordville, and Pine Plains. The Fishkill Valley and its "great milk region . . . and

also ore beds and marble quarries," would be deprived of a rail route to export their product and a chance to import coal directly from Pennsylvania. Construction would not begin until $500,000 [$17,256,089 in 2021 dollars] . . . was raised. (McDermott 21–22)

Brown made clear he wanted to be the principal capitalist close to the railroad, take stock in it, and control it for himself. To do so, he needed a half-million dollars to fund the railroad. The D&CRR was to be a railroad of the people, by the people, and for the people—if the people funded it for Brown. They did, and George Brown controlled it.

The State of New York issued a charter in September 1866 to the D&CRR to build a railroad from Plum Point (later Dutchess Junction) to the Connecticut state line. The D&CRR built tracks to the northwest of the hamlet of Hopewell and on to Millbrook. It planned to extend the tracks from Millbrook to Millerton and connect with the Connecticut and Western Railroad (C&WRR), which began laying tracks from Hartford, Connecticut, west to the New York State line near Millerton. The C&WRR eventually linked with the D&CRR. Thus, it formed a through route from north-central Connecticut to Pennsylvania (McLaughlin 7).

The first name change for the new D&CRR came before its first revenue run. In November 1868, the D&CRR sold about eleven miles of their track, from Plum Point to northwest of the hamlet of Hopewell, to the Boston, Hartford & Erie Railroad (BH&ERR) for $100,000.00. The reason for the unexpected, abrupt sale is shrouded in mystery, according to William Mc Dermott. It appears that the D&CRR may have been in financial trouble, although railroad management denied this trouble with reassuring public remarks (23).

Prevented from building from Waterbury, Connecticut, to New York City by the New Haven Railroad and wanting, in turn, to prevent the C&WRR from accessing the Hudson River by connecting with the D&CRR, the BH&ERR planned to link with the Erie Railroad at Newburgh. To accomplish this plan, the BH&ERR bought the tracks of the D&CRR from northwest of the hamlet of Hopewell to the Hudson River. It also built ferry docks on Denning's Point, a peninsula in Dutchess County, located just north of Plum Point and across the river from Newburgh (McLaughlin 9).

Then, unexpectedly, in March 1870, the apparently successful BH&ERR failed. About midnight, on March 22, 1870, George H. Brown, still chairman of the board of the D&CRR, woke up fireman Roswell S. Judson. The pair got up steam in the engine called the *Washington* at Plum Point. By 2 a.m., they started for northwest of the hamlet of Hopewell. There, they gained control of a set of BH&ERR locomotives and cars by removing the rails of a spur track connecting the D&CRR track to a BH&ERR construction site and marooning the BH&ERR locomotives and cars on the severed spur. The D&CRR once again was in the transportation business. It purchased a locomotive and four passenger coaches and borrowed several other cars from the HRRR (Mc Dermott 29).

The D&CRR remained in business for three more years. It transported anthracite coal from Plum Point, produce and goods from Dutchess County, and passengers across Dutchess County to either the HRRR or the NY&HRR bound for New York City and Albany.

Aboard the Inaugural Run of the Boston, Hartford, and Erie Railroad

Despite the ownership controversies, on Monday, June 21, 1869, the first train departed Plum Point (later Dutchess Junction) and traveled east to Millbrook. The train was labeled the Boston, Hartford, and Erie Railroad (BH&ERR) because the BH&ERR not the D&CRR owned the track. The chocolate-colored coaches had lettered on their sides "BH&E Railroad." A reporter from the *Poughkeepsie Eagle* went aboard and wrote an account of the run, which was reprinted in the *Fishkill Standard*:

> The train consisted of the Taunton built locomotive "Regular No. 5," drawing a "Clove Branch Car" [a freight car for transporting iron], and one regular and nicely fitted up passenger car. The locomotive was gaily decorated with flags. [. . .] At 10:45 a.m. Conductor Bailey gave the starting signal, there was a rush of

tardy voyagers, and then down the Hudson River Road to the junction [Dutchess Junction] rattled the train. [. . .] [B]y Matteawan we went without stopping, and then came to Fishkill. Here a number got out of the cars, shook hands with friends, smiled patronizingly at the pretty telegraph operator, jumped aboard again, and in a moment the train was once more off. Hopewell Junction, and another brief halt, and then "on to Millbrook." Here another stop. Millbrook is growing finely. Last July there was nothing in the way of a store or a dwelling visible about the depot. Now can be seen a three-story brick hotel, a large store 28x62, [. . .] a two-story dwelling house, a large machine shop, [a] saw mill, and six other houses; also a brick tin shop 24x72 [. . .]. Here, too, is a fine brick building with [a] French roof, in which is located the main office of the Dutchess & Columbia Railroad Company. The telegraph operator, Miss Georgie Preston, has an office in the really very pretty little passenger house. The station agent is Mr. A. T. Merritt [. . . .] After a short delay, the train again started, passing Shunpike, Stissing, and Attlebury, without stopping, reaching Pine Plains at 12:43 noon. As the excursion was a private one, there was no public reception. [. . .]

From Millbrook to Pine Plains it is fourteen miles, and the track is ready for the iron four miles beyond the latter point. It is expected the road will be finished to Millerton fifteen miles further by spring. We have been told that the receipts of the new road thus far have doubled every month, and great haste is being made to add to the rolling stock. When completed through to Boston, the demand for coal along the entire route will be 2,000 tons daily, and other supplies will be needed.

Although this report mentions "Hopewell Junction and another brief halt," there was no "Hopewell Junction" at this time. The "old" hamlet of Hopewell was situated southeast of where the train stopped. The depot would not be built until about 1873, the "new" hamlet of Hopewell would not become settled until after it was built, and the "new" Hopewell did not become a junction until 1881. In short, the train appears to have "briefly halted" in the middle of nowhere in particular.

The report also mentions female telegraphers. The D&CRR or the BH&ERR employed women—as well as men—to work at the stations and to communicate via telegraph between stations and among the cities, towns, and villages in which the stations were located. Nancy Smiler Levinson observes in her book *She's Been Working on the Railroad*:

> Many women worked the Morse system on the railroad. Their count is not known because records were inaccurate and incomplete, but most women hired by railroad companies in the nineteenth century were telegraph operators. Operators were called brass pounders and later simply "ops." (5)

Levinson's remark about "inaccurate and incomplete" records that obscure the identity of the women railroad employees applies to the two women mentioned by the *Poughkeepsie Eagle* correspondent. The first is described as "pretty" but remains unnamed, and the second is named but otherwise unknown. In addition, the few remaining records of the BH&ERR as well as of the D&CRR, are incomplete in terms of employee names and their payrolls.

The reporter also commented on the rapid development of the village of Millbrook. Within a year, houses and shops were built and open for occupancy. A similar, relatively quick development of a hamlet around a station occurred at the new hamlet of Hopewell.

Two Hamlets Named Hopewell: Not a Junction in Sight

The small, scattered, rural community settlement called Hopewell emerged from the wilderness and was focused on the Dutch Reformed Church founded there in 1757. This Hopewell consisted of farms; cider, grain, and lumber mills; several residences palatial and plain; a schoolhouse built about 1820; and a post office built in 1828. They all were located at or about the intersection of cart paths and wagon trails, now known as the intersection of the Beekman and the Clove Branch roads (Mills 9).

"Old" Hopewell Dutch Reformed Church. The Dutch Reformed Church in East Fishkill, New York, and the location of "Old" Hopewell, New York. The viewpoint is from what is now named the Beekman Road. The original post office of Hopewell was located across the street from the church on what is now named the Clove Branch Road. Photograph Courtesy of the East Fishkill Historical Society.

The D&CRR built tracks in 1868 located on land northwest of "Old" Hopewell. Between 1868 and 1873, the D&CRR constructed a relatively large station next to those tracks close enough to Hopewell rather than to any other settlement for the railroad to designate it as the Hopewell depot. The center of "Old" Hopewell shifted from the Dutch Reformed Church to the depot itself, from the congregational center to the commercial center. An example of that shift is the relocation of the Hopewell post office (the service not the building) from the intersection of the now named Beekman and Clove Branch roads to 7 Railroad Avenue, just up the street from the Hopewell depot. The post office was moved to accommodate both the railroad and the growing number of residents now living in the houses in and around the Hopewell depot. The railroad delivered and picked up mail at the depot through the Railway mail service.

In *Niwot Colorado: Birth of a Railroad Town*, Anne Quinby Dyni describes the beginning of a similar settlement influenced by a railroad: "Few records remain of those early buildings. [H]istoric photographs reveal stores and a few residences tucked among the trees. [. . .] The stores were wooden or brick. [. . .] [O]nly horse-drawn wagons and buggies travelled the roads [. . .]" (Dyni 39–40).

The first known photograph of the new Hopewell depot was taken in about 1901. It shows several buildings including the Hopewell Inn; the Hopewell post office; the Borden Creamery; as well as wide dirt roads; tracks; the telegraph/telephone poles that followed the tracks; and the

"New" Hopewell Junction Post Office. The building is a residential home at 7 Railroad Avenue. Photograph Courtesy of the East Fishkill Historical Society.

freight cars themselves at rest. From this picture, we can deduce that, between 1873 and 1901, roads were built from Madame Brett's Highway (now Route 82) to the depot, then alongside and traveling away from it. These roads eventually were named as Center Street, Railroad Avenue, and Bridge Street, respectively, by 1901. The second floors of the shops provided lodging for the single men who worked primarily on the railroad either as section gangs repairing track or later as junction crews performing the several tasks of a junction itself, such as repairing and storing extra locomotives and freight and passenger cars. As the single men became married men and family men, more residences were built not only along the streets but also along what has become Route 82 and some side streets leading from 82. The depot became a meeting place for the growing number of residents of the emerging hamlet to discuss the development of their community.

Railroad Avenue, Hopewell Junction, New York. The viewpoint is east down Railroad Avenue. In the foreground on the right side of the frame sits the Hopewell Junction depot at its original location at the corner of Bridge Street and Railroad Avenue. The white building behind the depot is Borden's Creamery. On the left side of the frame is the Hopewell Inn, and two buildings down is the Hopewell Junction post office. Photograph from the Private Collection of Bernard L. and Celeste Rudberg, Courtesy of Celeste Rudberg.

"Junction" is usually and specifically a railroad term meaning an intersection of tracks and a connection of railroads, perhaps operated by different companies. By that narrow definition, Hopewell did not become a junction until 1881 when the Newburgh, Dutchess, and Columbia Railroad (ND&CRR) intersected with the New York and New England Railroad (NY&NERR), coming from Danbury, Connecticut, northwest to "New" Hopewell. Yet "junction" typically, and generally refers to any intersection of roads, planned or actual, rail or hard-packed dirt. As late as 1870, the BH&ERR planned a rail line from Waterbury, Connecticut, west to what became "New" Hopewell to intersect with the D&CRR, making Hopewell a junction.

The BH&ERR never built the proposed line; instead, it bought the line of the D&CRR and then went bankrupt within two years. Thus, the wide definition of "junction" may to some narrow extent explain the reason the BH&ERR used the name "Hopewell Junction" on its timetables from 1869 to 1870 even though no other railroad intersected the D&CRR at Hopewell then. Thus, too, the reporter from the *Poughkeepsie Eagle* called the place at which the train stopped "Hopewell Junction."

The Hub of the Hamlet: The Hopewell Depot Circa 1873

The focus of the hamlet of "New" Hopewell was the depot. The Hopewell depot is one of the largest stations built by the D&CRR. Its size suggests it may have been designed to be an essential location for railroad activity between Mattawan (now Beacon) and Millbrook on the D&CRR line.

The exact date when the D&CRR built the depot has been difficult to determine. Unfortunately for railroad historians, all the known records of the D&CRR were destroyed when the joint stations of the New York Central and Hudson Railroad (NYC&HRR) and the D&CRR at Dutchess Junction burned to the ground in 1876. All present accounts of the D&CRR come from newspaper articles written contemporaneous with the railroad itself, and so far, no preserved article from these newspapers mentions the building of the depot.

Nonetheless, by comparing the Beers maps from 1867 and 1878, the D&CRR must have built the Hopewell depot sometime between these two dates. The 1867 Beers map shows neither a railroad nor a station at Hopewell, while the 1878 Beers map shows both. For no factual reason but for a useful explanation, Dutchess County historians (see Mills 81), including Bernard Rudberg and this author, practically split the difference between these two dates, to circa 1873.

The 1878 Beers map shows only the general location of the railroad and the depot. Its exact location is first documented in its earliest known photograph dated circa 1901.

The designers of the early railroad stations in Dutchess County were mindful of the influence of the Dutch Colonial style of architecture in the Hudson Valley. Such touches as Jerkin-Head gables and basket-handle arches above the windows and (at one time) above all four of the doors of the depot reflect this architectural tradition. A boardwalk continues all the way around the depot with the roof extending over it to shelter bystanders and freight from bad weather.

The floor plan of the depot includes two passenger waiting rooms separated by a corridor. Off the corridor on one side is a station-agent's office. The station agent supervised freight deliveries and pickups. On the other side of the corridor is a telegraph office with two ticket windows on either side of this office, each one facing a different waiting room. A baggage-storage area is also in the telegraph office. The telegraph office eventually included a telephone. The telegraph-telephone operator also sold tickets to passengers.

A telegraph message dated February 11, 1884, issued instructions to send equipment and supplies to the Hopewell depot to paint the building. Pigments included ochre yellow for the outside walls, chocolate brown for the doors and window frames, white for the interior walls, and sky blue for the ceiling. Whether these colors were typical for railroad stations built by the D&CRR and later maintained by the ND&CRR is unknown. How often stations were repainted is also unknown. This telegraph message provides the color scheme that was followed by the restorers of the depot.

The Ending of the Dutchess and Columbia Railroad

In 1873, the D&CRR suffered financial losses because of insufficient income from transporting freight and passengers through Dutchess County and the Financial Panic of 1873. A "financial panic" is a depression; before the Great Depression of 1929–39 outdated it, the Financial Panic of 1873 was called the Great Depression. The Panic of 1873 was caused in great part by the British investment in United States railroads, especially from 1865 to 1873 (Wolmar 124).

In *Passage to Union: How the Railroads Transformed American Life, 1829–1929*, Sarah H. Gordon explains that the collapse of the railroads, thus of the banks, and eventually of investors' funds, "was caused in part by building more railroads than any other town or state would need—in order to make money on financial speculation, without regard for the future usefulness of each line" (74–75).

Reflecting on the Panic of 1873, Cornelius Vanderbilt judged, "There are many worthless railroads started in this country without any means to carry them through. Building railroads from nowhere to nowhere at public expense is not a legitimate undertaking. Mistrust will be engendered till we, as a nation, do our business on a more solid basis, and pay as we go" (Hiltzik 85–86).

The D&CRR may not seem a railroad "from nowhere to nowhere" to the residents of Dutchess County, either in 1873 or today. Yet, to Vanderbilt, who built and controlled railroads that spanned much of the country from somewhere to somewhere, the short-haul railroad lines were insignificant local businesses that generated small amounts of money and that quickly went bankrupt.

Vanderbilt is not alone in disapproving the short-haul, railroads including those that ran through Dutchess County. D. W. McLaughlin comments that, "[a] scant 75 miles from the heart of Manhattan Island are two counties [Dutchess and Columbia] where 34 railroads were charted to serve a population of less than a 100,000 people—where nine of them were actually built to operate for many years before joining into one and ultimately ending up on the junk pile of history" (6).

This book sorts through that "junk pile." It extracts from the heap the various histories of these several individual, east-west, short-haul railroads. It restores their histories, both the successes and the failures, as a genuine and justifiable legacy for the two counties through which they once ran.

In 1874, the D&CRR foreclosed—only four years after its first run through Dutchess County. The railroad continued to run for three years more until 1877 under the direction of a court order. On August 5, 1876, a sale of the railroad's assets was held. John Crosby Brown bought the assets, and "Jon. Crosby Brown Trustee" was stenciled on all the old D&CRR rolling stock. Brown was the trustee of the First Mortgage Bond held on the D&CRR dating back to January 1, 1868 ("Mortgage").

In retrospect, the D&CRR and the Boston, Hartford, and Erie Railroad (BH&ERR) met at the beginning of their corporate lives all the requirements of what is needed to build a railroad as suggested by Christian Wolmar: vision, ambition, finances, permission of the state, legal framework, and labor. However, a lack of revenue and a nationwide depression with the D&CRR and over ambition with the BH&ERR ruined them.

The Beginning of the Newburgh, Dutchess, and Connecticut Railroad

In January 1877, a new corporation was formed, and the State of New York issued a charter for it under the name of the Newburgh, Dutchess and Connecticut Railroad (ND&CRR) (Haight 23). This new corporation took possession of the old D&CRR line in February 1877. Initially, the ND&CRR owned no rolling stock and rented well-used engines, tenders, and freight and passenger cars from the trustee of the D&CRR. Like many other short-line railroads, travel on the ND&CRR

> remained primitive. Whereas the larger railroad companies were, by the 1880s, introducing improvements such as electric lighting and steam heating on the trains, most passengers on these smaller lines did not see such progress until well into the twentieth century [. . .]. These short lines [. . .] tended to live off hand-me-downs from the larger companies, both locomotives and rolling stock (Wolmar 210).

Three of the ND&CRR's locomotives were wood burners that had been in service for over twenty years, and the cars used link-and-pin couplers and relied on hand-operated brakes. (A link-and-pin coupler is an early mechanism for joining railroad cars made up of a metal pin placed through a metal link.)

Health, Pleasure and Wealth

Can be found all along the line of

THE
Newburgh, Dutchess & Connecticut
RAILROAD

Where can you find purer air and water? Where more pleasant scenic effects and where more opportunities for locating to farm or to manufacture and so near the great markets too? It will pay you to interest yourself. Send two 2-cent stamps for our eighty page illustrated booklet, "Beautiful Dutchess County," describing the County from Dutchess Junction to Millerton, New York. ∴ ∴ ∴ ∴

The Newburgh, Dutchess & Connecticut R. R.

General Offices: **MATTEAWAN, N. Y.**

GENERAL OFFICERS:

John Crosby Brown, Pres. ..... 59 Wall St., N. Y.
G. Hunter Brown, Vice-Pres....Matteawan, N. Y.
W. A. Wells, Secretary .... "
H. H. Reed, Treas. and Gen. Acct. "
Wm. Underhill, Gen. Mgr. and
  Gen. Frt. and Pass Agt. .... "
A. C. Rapelje, Aud. Traffic Accts.. "

G. D. Holmes, Master Mechanic
    Dutchess Junction, N. Y.
R. P. Stanton, Road Master........Millbrook, N. Y.
Everett Garrison, Chief Engineer
    Newburgh, N. Y.
C. J. Conklin, Car Accountant
    Fishkill, N. Y.

Advertisement for the Newburgh, Dutchess, and Connecticut Railroad.

The *Washington* and Its Tender Crossing a Trestle. Photograph from the Private Collection of J. W. Swanberg, Courtesy of J. W. Swanberg.

Locomotives like the *Washington* often faced similar fates in the boom-bust world of short-haul railroads. The locomotive was built by Breese, Kneeland, and Company in 1856 for the East Tennessee and Virginia Railroad (ET&VRR). However, the ET&VRR defaulted on its payment for the locomotive, so it was sold to the Hampshire and Hamden Railroad (H&HRR) located in Massachusetts. The H&HRR, in turn, sold it to the D&CRR in 1869 for $4000.00. The *Washington* was delivered by barge to Dutchess Junction on February 15, 1869. The *Washington* burned wood and was never converted to burning coal.

After carrying George H. Brown and Roswell S. Judson from Plum Point up to Hopewell to gain control of the Boston, Hartford & Fishkill Railroad cars, the *Washington* toiled on the Clove Branch Railroad (CBRR) hauling iron ore out of the mine at Sylvan Lake. The locomotive was not powerful enough for that service, so it was advertised for sale in 1881. By that date, the D&CRR was out of business, and the *Washington* was owned by the ND&CRR. That railroad went shopping for a replacement for the *Washington*.

As the revenues of the ND&CRR increased, it purchased its own newer equipment. The revenue increases came primarily from transporting the iron ore from the mine at Sylvan Lake, the anthracite coal from the eastern Pennsylvania mines, and the milk from Dutchess County dairy farms. The ND&CRR survived through the good and bad economic times of the country for the next twenty-seven years, as the business letters and records of the railroad, known as the *Letter Books*, attest.

A Railroad Historian's Treasure:
The Letter Books of the Newburgh, Dutchess, and Connecticut Railroad

For those of us unfamiliar with the history of secretarial science, we ask: What is a letter book? The short answer is they are bound copies of business letters and records. Before the invention of copiers, computers, FAX machines, e-mails, and texts, these books enabled businesses to save and store duplicates of their correspondence and proceedings. Indeed, the early volumes of the ND&CRR letter books contain letters and records written by hand before the common use of typewriters in officers during the mid-1880s. That last fact conjures up images of Charles Dickens's Bob Cratchit, an office clerk who hunches over an oak desk carefully and dutifully writing out business correspondence or of Herman Melville's Bartleby, another office clerk, who "prefers not to" write out such correspondence.

After writing a business letter or filling out a record form, the clerk would make a copy of it using a method that included water and two pieces of paper. As Dr. Brian Davies explains:

> [t]he principle of [the] method was that a piece of very thin and un-sized paper was moistened and placed on top of the fresh writing. The two layers were squeezed together either in a screw press or in the roller press [. . .]. A portion of the ink was transferred from the original paper to the thin tissue; the writing was reversed as a mirror image, of course, but could easily be read from the other side as the paper was so thin.

The original was mailed, and the copy when dry was then bound into an eleven-by-seventeen-inch hardcover book to form a permanent file. The thin tissue paper of the copy allowed seven hundred pages in each volume.

Forty-eight volumes of the ND&C *Letter Books* survive. The earliest dated book is from 1879, when the railroad was just two years old. The last book is dated 1904, less than one year before the ND&C was absorbed into the Central New England Railroad (CNERR). The volumes were found by accident. The ND&C headquarters building was located on 493 Main Street, in Beacon, New York. In the 1990s, the building was renovated into stores and apartments, during which workers discovered the discarded *Letter Books*. A member of the Beacon Historical Society, Larry Way, learned of the discovery and donated the volumes to the society's archives. Some of the volumes in between 1879 and 1904 are missing. However, the surviving volumes give us a rich insight into the business of running a railroad in the last two decades of the nineteenth and the first few years of the twentieth centuries.

More than just a primary source of the day-to-day operation of the railroad, the *Letter Books* paint an immediate vivid picture of the people, both extraordinary and commonplace, who made it all happen. The books allow us glimpses into a by-gone railroad world from the 1880s up to the early 1900s.

The first two volumes of the surviving *Letter Books* cover the railroad's operations for most of 1879. This correspondence focuses on the problem of running a railroad with equipment that some other railroad owned. Mentioned in several records and letters are lists of locomotives and cars used by the ND&CRR but owned by the trustees of the ND&CRR.

Maintenance of this rolling stock posed a problem. There is a copy of a letter dated April 9, 1879, from the ND&CRR's general manager, Charles L. Kimball, to the attorney for the trustees, James Lawry. Kimball requests Lawry to arrange for needed repairs of Engine #6 before putting the engine into service. Lawry at some time approved to have Engine #6 repaired by the NY&HRR in Millerton, New York. Nearly seven weeks after Kimball's request to Lawry, Kimball sends a note to Lawry dated May 27 advising him that the said engine would be forwarded to Millerton for repairs: "Will forward engine six tomorrow morning to Millerton. Will Robert's man receive her there or should I send man to Brewster [NY] & deliver and get receipt there? Signed C. L. Kimball."

An unsigned receipt dated the next day, May 28, shows Engine #6 was forwarded and received: "Received from the Newburgh, Dutchess, and Connecticut Railroad Co. One (1) locomotive-being NYC&HRR Ry No.

Engine #6 and Its Tender and Crew. Photograph from the Private Collection of J. W. Swanberg, Courtesy of J. W. Swanberg.

6-in good order together with the following tools belonging to said engine." The tools included a coal scoop, coal pick, jacks, wrenches, and flags.

Being received is no guarantee of being repaired. Four months after Engine #6 reached Millerton, it still had not been repaired because of indecision over whether it could be mended in Millerton or needed to be sent on to Schenectady, New York. Whatever the reason(s) for the long lapses between the Kimball-Lawry correspondence and for the indecision to repair Engine #6, Christian Wolmar emphasizes that

> [u]niquely, running a railroad involved a myriad of vital and often safety-critical decisions to be made daily, often by quite junior staff. Working out the requirements of each station and freight depot and allocating the right resources and monitoring performance were new tasks [. . .]. (230)

In short, Lawry, the man who received Engine #6, the mechanics who did or did not repair the engine, and even Kimball, who was a veteran railroad man, were all still learning on the job. Gaps in communication and gaffes in performance occurred. Engine #6 is never mentioned again in the *Letter Books*. Yet above is a photograph of it, its tender, and its crew.

Chapter 3

Glimpses into the Standard Operating Procedures of a Short-Haul Railroad

The *Letter Books* of the ND&CRR

The *Letter Books* cover many operational subjects of the ND&CRR, including Dutchess Junction, Fishkill Landing, Buying and Selling Equipment, Bridges, the Coal Business, the Milk Business, Coping with the Weather, and the Lighter Side of Railroading.

The First Port of Call: Dutchess Junction

Many of the letters in the *Letter Books* are between President Schultze and Superintendent Kimball. Kimball reports to Schultze events on the line or asks Schultze for management decisions on major plans for the line. For example, Schultze wrote Kimball for some information about the history of Dutchess Junction. Kimball wrote a lengthy description detailing activities and buildings located there.

Around 1873, an unknown artist sketched the joint stations of the New York Central and Hudson River Railroad (NYC&RR) and the former D&CRR and eventually the ND&CRR at Dutchess Junction. The artist's viewpoint looks north. In the background lies Fishkill Landing (now Beacon). In the middle ground and to the left stretches Denning's Point, extending out into the Hudson River. In the center middle ground stands the trestle over the NYC&HRRR tracks and the pilings for a trestle over a cove of the Hudson River leading to Denning's Point built and then abandoned by the failed Boston, Hartford, and Fishkill Railroad. In the foreground, the ND&CRR tracks veer off to the right and up the hill to the Tioronda Bridge and Wicopee Junction. (In the drawing, "Tioronda" refers to the Tioronda Bridge spanning over the Fishkill Creek. "Wicopee" refers to Wicopee Junction, a location, not a community, where a switch joining the tracks of the ND&CRR and the NY&NERR was located.) The arch framing the foreground of the drawing is the station roof shared by both railroads exiting over the NYC&HRRR double track, the ND&CRR main track, and one ND&CRR siding.

The building burned to the ground in 1876, three years after the drawing and eight years before Kimball wrote his 1884 letter to Schultze. Unfortunately for railroad historians, all the known records of the D&CRR burned with the building. Kimball's description drew primarily on his memory of the stations. For years to come, the ND&CRR had to rely on the Kimball's memories and the memories of others concerning questions about the D&CRR.

According to Kimball, from 1877 until 1883, Dutchess Junction was the center of activity for the ND&CRR. It thrived as the junction of the ND&CRR and the NYC&HRRR. It featured a busy dock for ferries carrying both freight and passengers up, down, and across the Hudson River. It included the ND&CRR repair services consisting of a brass foundry, a carpenter shop, a car repair and build shop, a local coal pocket (an overhead container for the storage and distribution of coal into the coal tenders of steam locomotives parked directly below the pocket), a locomotive shop, a paint shop, a rail yard, a turntable, and a water tower. Adjacent to the rail yards stood a brick-manufacturing company. Scattered around Dutchess Junction were tenement houses owned by the ND&CRR, where their railroad workers lived.

At Dutchess Junction, the ND&CRR had a problem accessing the ferry dock. The dock was located on the west side of the NYC&HRR tracks. Only a narrow strip of land lay between those tracks and the river. Passengers exited the ferries, walked across the narrow strip of land, went into the station, and entered either a ND&CRR or a NYC&HRR train.

However, carloads of coal and other types of freight had to be loaded onto freight cars for transportation first on a D&CRR train and then later a ND&CRR train. This required ND&CRR trains to cross over the double main line of the NYC&HRR to reach the dock and the ferry freight and to recross the double main line to reach the ND&CRR tracks again. This operation required intricate switching of rails and careful management of time to avoid possible damaging or fatal accidents.

In November 1893, the roundhouse, timber shed, store house, and the timbers supporting the water tank burned:

> When the fire broke out, George Washington, obviously not the president but certainly an employee of the ND&CRR, saved one of the locomotives. According to Inglis Stuart, in *The Dutchess and Columbia R.R. and Its Associates*, "[Washington] was advanced in years and by no means as agile as formerly but he had quick perception and, despite the rapidity with which the flames spread, he managed to run No. 1 to a place of safety. The other housed locomotives were reduced to hulks and it took a long time to restore them."

Stewart also mentions that Washington was an emancipated slave employed by the ND&CRR. After the Civil War, Blacks were hired to work track building and maintenance and permitted to be fireman and brakemen but not engineers. Steward does not mention if Washington was a fireman, but for him to be able to run an engine, he had to have some knowledge of getting up steam, sliding the throttle, and pulling the break lever. Whatever Washington's occupation, he needed quick perception, self-possession, and locomotive skills required of all engineers whether in an emergency or on a routine run.

The Second Port of Call: Fishkill Landing

By 1881, major changes occurred in the operation of the ND&CRR at Hopewell. A new railroad for "New" Hopewell, the NY&NERR, finished building tracks from Danbury, Connecticut, northwest to "New" Hopewell.

This event made "New" Hopewell a railroad junction. The NY&NERR shared with the ND&CRR the one-track line from "New" Hopewell to the Hudson River authorized by a lease with the ND&CRR.

The NY&NERR opened a passenger- and freight-ferry service larger than the one at Dutchess Junction and located approximately two miles north at Fishkill Landing (now Beacon). The ferries transported train cars from the terminal of the Newburgh Branch of the Erie Railroad across the Hudson River to the terminal of the NY&NERR. The ferry service featured a brand new, large, and powerful railroad-car ferry christened the *William T. Hart*. The *Hart* was powered by two complete steam engines and was sailed by a crew of twenty-four men. The *Hart* was much more efficient compared with the smaller car floats used by the ND&CRR at Dutchess Junction.

The NY&NERR train left the dock, traveled along a newly constructed line, crossed the tracks of the NYC&HRRR on an overhead bridge to avoid traffic conflicts with the other railroad, and continued to Wicopee Junction. There the NY&NERR train switched over to the ND&CRR line for the eleven-mile trip to Hopewell Junction. At Hopewell Junction, NY&NERR

Fishkill Landing. Photograph Courtesy of Beacon Historical Society.

train switched over to its track and turned southeast to Danbury. The two docks, the two sets of tracks, and the two railroads coexisted to 1904.

A track and the bridge are still there. One can park a car in one of the lots at Long Dock just to the south of the Metro-North Beacon station and walk the broad dirt path south to Denning's Point. As one walks along, one can notice the track to the left. It seems to rise out of the bushes and small trees. The neglected track eventually becomes free of the undergrowth and emerges through a Metro-North Railroad fence gate to run closely parallel to the path. One can walk on the track from that point on. Just before the path reaches a T-intersection with the road leading to a private residence, a factory under restoration, the path out to Denning's Point, and the Clarkson University Hudson River Extension, the track curves to the left. It crosses the road at grade level and goes onto the bridge. Once across the bridge, the track leads to the former site of Wicopee Junction.

The management of the ND&CRR saw the advantages of a bridge crossing over a switch crossing. Within two years, in 1883, the ND&CRR coal freight that crossed the Hudson River traveled on the *Hart* to the NY&NERR dock at Fishkill Landing. The ND&CRR trains picked up their coal cars, traveled on the NY&NERR line and bridge over the NYC&HRR tracks, and switched at Wicopee Junction to their own tracks for the trip up to Hopewell, by now a junction.

The ND&C no longer needed as many car floats at Dutchess Junction, so the pace of business at that dock slowed considerably. Barge and passenger-ferry traffic continued; passengers still boarded NYC&HRR and ND&CRR trains; the switches still operated for the ND&CRR trains crossing the NYC&HRR tracks; and local freight was still handled.

Today, Dutchess Junction exists only on maps of Dutchess County as a place situated south of Denning's Point and the Fishkill Creek within Fishkill. It forms part of the Hudson Highlands State Park. When Bernard Rudberg asked residents where Dutchess Junction was located, they responded with a puzzled look. Rudberg found the nearest passable road more than a mile from where he thought the junction had been located. From the road, he hiked through the woods to where he came upon a few overgrown foundations and some scattered bricks. He heard Metro-North and Amtrak trains thunder past him in the woodland along the banks of the Hudson River. Although owned and operated by totally different railroads in totally different times from the ND&CRR and the NYC&HRRR, the train's whoosh and whistle are all that suggests the vanished railroad culture among the crumbled ruins of Dutchess Junction.

Buying and Selling Equipment

Most of the ND&CRR equipment in the early years of the railroad's history was inherited from the previous railroad, the D&CRR. The earliest *Letter Books* chronicle buying replacements for the old, worn-out D&CRR equipment and, in turn, selling the older units, sometimes only for scrap. Probably the best example of the purchasing process is for the old D&CRR locomotive *Washington*. The process by which it eventually was sold, as told in the *Letter Books*, was a complex—convoluted—process. Kimball first wrote on April 18, 1881, to J. Ralph, the superintendent of the Freehold & NY (F&NY) Railroad describing the engine:

> Making a statement of what repairs the engine would require which I will send to you as soon as prepared, I think the engine would answer for a light train on your road very nicely—she is smart [meaning well-maintained] and doing good work on the C.B. [Clove Branch] Road but is not heavy or powerful enough for the business of that road when both [iron] furnaces are in blast. She ought in my judgement (sic) to be worth $3000 as she stands. Come up and look at her and we will talk the matter up fully-what is your maximum grade? (Volume 12, page 3)

On April 29, Kimball made a sensible, straight-forward, inviting sales pitch to Ralph:

> In reply to your favor of the 12th, we will sell you the engine Washington of the CBRR just as she stands for $2500 provided we can procure another engine to take her place within a reasonable time. I make this proviso for the reason that the shops are busy and if we had to rent an engine for several months

before a new one could be procured, we might better keep the Washington. [. . .] In case you wish to take the Washington at the above price which I think is fair for both companies, Mr. Van Buskirk advises that main valves need facing, etc. etc, [list of needed repairs itemized here]. These repairs he estimates would cost from $50 to $75 and with them the engine should run years on a light train with ordinary roundhouse repairs that any engine might need. (Volume 12, page 52)

On May 3, Kimball reduced the asking price and lists the engine's needed repairs as part of his negotiation strategy:

Replying to your favor of yesterday I have to say that I have asked the Baldwin Locomotive Works, the Rogers Locomotive and Machine Works and the Danforth Locomotive and Machine Company to name prices and earliest date of delivery possible for such a locomotive as we want and asked them to answer at once. As soon as I hear from them, I will advise by telegraph to save time stating whether or not we will part with the Washington. There are two Westinghouse brakes on fixtures for them here? (Volume 12, page 63)

In these letters, Kimball has been writing not exclusively as a businessman but partially as Ralph's friend. Kimball includes chatty comments about buying a house and who has been married and died. But Kimball's tone suddenly changes in his next letter written to Ralph on May 5, addressing him formally and distantly as "Dear Sir" and informing him of the bad news:

Dear Sir, Today's mail brings word for those locomotive builders-Grant cannot deliver an engine before February 1882. Danforth Locomotive and Machine Co. will not name a date-Rogers Locomotive and Machine Works named March 1882. None of these will name a price now. Have not heard from Baldwin. It does not look like we can spare the Washington. (Volume 12, page 85)

Ralph's response appears lost. Two months later, on July 31, 1881, Kimball tried to sell the *Washington* to a used equipment dealer in New York City:

> Gents, the Washington is still unsold, price the same, but sale must be contingent upon our being able to supply her place with a new double-end engine of greater capacity.
>
> In case you wish to purchase her, advise me, and I will see how soon we can get a new engine built. (Volume 12, page 374)

Meanwhile, the *Washington* worked hard pulling iron-ore cars out of the Sylvan Lake mine. In a letter written on September 26, 1881, to ND&CRR President John L. Schultze, Kimball explains the condition of the *Washington* and the reasons why the locomotive is in the shop for repairs:

> We will need another engine to take [the Washington's] place and keep her here until the new flues have been put in and her valves put in order. H. Lasher either by carelessness or ignorance twisted one of the steam pipes in the engine that was sent up to take the place of the Washington, rendering it necessary to retain the engine to fix the joint. We are short of power at present and have been for several days but will be alright in a day or two. Lasher is inclined not to give the Washington a fair chance, I fear. In fact, I don't think much of his ability anyway. (Volume 12, page 562)

Kimball expresses his frustration at the mechanics responsible for keeping the *Washington* running while the sale of the underpowered locomotive drags on too long. In March 29, 1883, the need for a new locomotive increased drastically, according to a memorandum Kimball wrote to Schultze describing a major accident on the Clove Branch Railroad involving—once more—the *Washington*:

> At 3:05 PM March 15th [the engine *Washington* left] the main track between the two siding switches at Sylvan Lake. The tender left the rails first and when the engine was stopped not

more than fifty [feet] from where it left the rails, the forward truck [wheel] of the tender was under the rear pair of drivers of the engine and the whole of the tender and the rest of the drivers of the engine remained on the rail OK. The engine was backing at the time. The track at this point was perfect and I cannot account for the truck of the tender leaving the rail unless something from the truck may have dropped and obstructed the wheels.

The engine is very badly wrecked both pumps being broken, ash pan demolished, engine frame bent, and I fear one driving axel bent, spring hangers all broken, tender truck demolished and otherwise there are many little things broken. I hardly think it will ever pay us to repair her. There was no damage to the cars in the train. (Volume 16, pages 113–14)

Kimball does not mention any injury to the crew. Now the lack of a new more powerful locomotive became critical. There was no replacement locomotive on order, and cars full of iron ore waited at the Sylvan Lake mine. Within a few days of Kimball's memorandum, he wrote several letters to other railroads and locomotive dealers inquiring if there was another locomotive immediately available for sale. The Baldwin Locomotive Works offered a locomotive for $8,250.00, with a delivery of October 1883; the Rogers Locomotive Works offered a locomotive for $8.000.00, with a delivery of August 1883. The Rogers bid was enthusiastically accepted, and Baldwin's bid was politely rejected.

Volume 17 of the *Letter Books* is missing, so there are no known records from August 1883 to January 1884. The next mention of the new Rogers locomotive is February 2, 1884, when it had been in service for about six months. Kimball reported that several rails on the CBRR broke under the weight of the new locomotive, which was heavier than the old *Washington*. Kimball decided to replace all the brittle, weaker iron rails with stronger steel rails. The iron was sold for scrap.

The *Washington*'s fate remains uncertain today. The ND&CRR received a check in April 1884 for $500.00 from John J. Hurley in payment for the locomotive. What Hurley did with it is unknown.

The Ups and Downs of Bridges

The ND&CRR also inherited its bridges from its bankrupt predecessor. Nearly all were designed and built for light-duty, slow-moving locomotives and cars; these wooden structures could not support the strain exerted by heavier locomotives and cars traveling at relatively higher rates of speed. Over the 25 years of ND&CRR operation chronicled in the *Letter Books*, the railroad replaced just about all the wooden bridges with iron and steel spans capable of supporting the heavier, faster trains.

One overworked wooden bridge was the Tioronda, the longest, highest bridge on the railroad. The Tioronda crossed the Fishkill Creek ravine in Mattawan (now Beacon) from lofty, rocky abutments. The bridge-painting crew reported the bridge's nuts and bolts as being either loose or missing. Were the Tioronda to collapse, it, the unfortunate locomotive, the ill-fated cars, and especially the star-crossed crew would make a spectacular, disastrous splash.

Track crews added more bolts and stronger brace rods to bolster the Tioronda. Fire-proof paint covered the wooden ties and pilings to

The Tioranda Bridge over the Fishkill Creek in Mattawan (now Beacon), after 1876. Courtesy of the Beacon Historical Society.

prevent blazes. These increased maintenance measures worked to preserve the bridge for a time. However, the trains running over them kept getting heavier, faster, and more frequent. By the early 1890s, the ND&CRR began a much-needed bridge-replacement program.

This long-range project began with several letters to the Phoenix Bridge Company in Philadelphia. Since the Tioranda Bridge replacement was a big project, the ND&CRR asked the Phoenix to accept a ninety-day note in place of the payment due on completion of the new bridge. The completion date was the end of May 1896, so the Phoenix agreed to accept the note as partial payment on June 2.

On June 11, the ND&CRR conducted a test of the new bridge. Although the railroad used one of its lighter locomotives and tenders, it filled both with water, coal, and even pig iron (a crude form of iron that is an intermediate product in the process of producing steel). The grand total of weight was 165,700 pounds. The test proved successful, so eight days later, on June 19, the chief engineer for the ND&CRR signed a statement that certified the Tioranda Bridge had passed all tests and was officially accepted by the railroad. The railroad then sent the ninety-day payment note to the Phoenix.

A few months later, the ND&CRR discovered the Phoenix had not done as a good a job as it should have. The bridge had been built with undersized anchor bolts. The bolts measured half the size called for in the specifications ordered by the railroad. The ND&CRR was dissatisfied. It is not known how the issue was resolved because volumes 45, 46, and 47 of the *Letter Books* are missing.

Five years after the Tioranda Bridge was built, in 1901, the approaches to the bridge proved to be too weak for the newer, heavier locomotives purchased to handle the increased coal traffic. As a precaution, the ND&CRR management advised their conductors to watch out for heavy cars and not to couple these cars close to the locomotive. This practice would distribute the weight of the locomotive and tender as well as the other cars when they crossed the approaches.

Notwithstanding precautions, the ND&CRR continued to worry about the Tioranda Bridge. In early 1902, the management of the railroad wanted to replace the bridge with a still stronger structure. The Phoenix wanted to build the new bridge for $12,000. That quote was $3,500 too much for the management; therefore, they decided not to pursue the matter further.

The heavier trains still strained the bridge, so more stringers were installed to strengthen the span, and a four-mile-an-hour speed limit for freight trains was enforced. The Pennsylvania Railroad (PRR) offered the ND&CRR one span of a double-track bridge, but the ND&CRR could not find a company that would modify the bridge to fit its requirements. As a result, that offer was dropped.

However, weak as it was, the Tioranda Bridge never collapsed, remained in service, and eventually was scrapped in 1916, twenty years after it was built. The remaining abutment of the bridge can be seen in the Madame Brett Park on the Fishkill Creek in Beacon. These aging bridges, their successors, or at least their weather-scoured abutments can be found today at their various creek, river, and stream sites. They are tangible and specific remnants and reminders of the ND&CRR, bygone now in 2022 for 117 years.

As with nearly all construction projects, annoying yet humorous incidents occurred. The wooden guard rails for the Sprout Creek Bridge did not arrive on time because they had been left on a dock in Jacksonville, Florida.

Transporting Coal—Most of the Time

ND&CRR assumed ownership of the bankrupt D&CRR, it resumed its predecessor's business of transporting anthracite coal. In the exchange of railroad companies and their initials, there had been no interruption in the flow of anthracite coal from the dock of the Penn Coal Company at Newburgh across the Hudson River on car-float ferries to the dock of D&CRR and now the ND&CRR at Dutchess Junction. The car floats had built-in tracks on their decks that fitted directly and tightly with the tracks on the docks, so train cars could be rolled on and off the floats. This supply chain was supplemented by barges carrying anthracite coal from the terminus of the Delaware and Hudson Canal at Kingston.

As the train moved along the ND&CRR line, it stopped in every hamlet, town, and village where a retail dealer bought coal and a factory used coal. The retail dealers, in turn, sold their coal to homeowners and other local businesses that did not buy coal directly from the ND&CRR.

Hauling coal presented its own potential dangers. Something as simple as the grade on a customer's siding posed a problem, as this notice from July 11, 1892, to engineers noted:

> Do not under any circumstances enter the Howard Haight and Co. coal track in Millbrook except with the engine headed east. The grade of this track is equal to 4-inch rise in 11 feet of track, and should you back your engine onto this siding you would bare the crown sheet and damage it. (Volume 34, page 51)

The crown sheet is located at the top of the firebox on steam locomotives. It should always be covered by water. If not covered by water, the crown sheet melts, and the locomotive's boiler could explode.

In the fall of 1887, a major bottleneck developed in the flow of coal from Newburgh to Dutchess Junction and Fishkill Landing. The ferry slip in the yard of the Newburgh Branch of the Erie Railroad needed to be rebuilt. In Dutchess County, coal was in short supply as homeowners and factory owners began stockpiling in anticipation of winter. On the dock at Dutchess Junction, hoists strained to lift as much coal as possible, about 100 tons per day, out of the barges and into train cars. Crews of men were recruited to speed up this process by shoveling coal from barge to

The Ferry William Hart. Photograph Courtesy of Beacon Historical Society.

car. Finally, the ferry slip was rebuilt, and gradually over the winter, coal supplies were satisfactorily replenished by homeowners and factory owners.

During the winter of 1888, one of the car floats, the large steamship *William T. Hart*, broke down. It remained in dry dock to be fixed. Again, a bottleneck developed in Newburgh, and coal supplies diminished. On March 11, 1888, the Great Blizzard began in the Hudson Valley and across the Northeast. It lasted three days, until March 14, made train traffic impassible, and reduced coal supplies even more.

Transporting Clean, Cold, Pure Farm Milk

During the nineteenth century, the population of American cities increased. The inhabitants' desire for high-quality milk not-so-obviously increased also. In *Milk Trains and Traffic*, Jeff Wilson explains why they desired high-quality milk,

> Although some cows were kept in large cities, the lack of grazing fields and low-quality feed they were given (often spent mash from breweries) resulted in 'swill milk,' which often had an off-taste and odor—and that was even when it was fresh. Customers much preferred 'country milk' from cows grazed on grass in pastures. (4)

How was the raw milk to get from the country to the city, from farm to table? Not by horse and wagon, Wilson declares. Before pasteurization, hermetical sealing, and refrigeration were developed and widely practiced, raw milk could not be transported by horse and wagon. It was better immediately churned into butter and cheese.

In the 1880s, the process of pasteurization became widespread. Pasteurization is the process of applying heat of up to 212 degrees Fahrenheit to foods and beverages, such as wine or, in the case of this book, raw milk, to destroy the pathogens in it that cause spoilage and illness. Once the milk had undergone pasteurization, it was hermetically sealed in bottles. Hermetical sealing is pouring the pasteurized milk into air-tight bottles to safeguard even more against spoilage. After the milk was hermetically sealed in bottles, it had to be kept cold with ice until a train arrived to transport the milk to dealers and from them to household ice boxes and kitchen tables. The processes of pasteurization, hermetically sealing, and refrigeration were done in creameries.

The ice often came from ponds located on farms. In the winter, when farming slowed down, the relatively idle farmers cut thick slabs of ice from their ponds and sold the blocks to local creameries. The farmers also sold hay to the creameries in which to pack the ice to keep it cold. One such creamery was Borden's Creamery located in Hopewell Junction and right next to the depot.

Another major revenue source for the ND&CRR was transporting milk. The railroad used two milk cars that ran the length of the line and back each day. These "milk cars," or "can cars," were wooden boxcars or baggage cars attached to passenger trains. Passenger trains provided better service for picking up raw milk rather than freight trains because they traveled at a faster rate and more-or-less kept to a set schedule. Time was of the essence for passengers and raw milk. (The term "milk train" derives from these early morning trains that during this period of railroading slowly made their way past the dairy farms and railroad stations on their way to a creamery for pasteurization and bottling. Today, a "milk train" is usually a commuter-railroad train that stops at every station along the line picking up its regular customers.)

A standard milk container, or can, held forty quarts, or ten gallons, of milk. Dairy farmers filled the cans with raw milk and placed them on specially built platforms located next to the tracks, either at railroad stations or on platforms constructed on the farms themselves and next to the tracks. These platforms remind one of the backyard decks frequently found outside the sliding-glass doors of houses today.

Weather and traffic delays sometimes delayed milk trains. Snow often filled the tracks between the Connecticut state line and Hopewell and blocked the trains until work crews shoveled the tracks clear again. In this circumstance, raw milk could neither be picked up nor delivered and may well have had to be churned into butter and cheese at the farm or it would have spoiled in the milk cans. Stalled and late trains occasionally held up traffic until the bottleneck could be cleared with the same results for the raw milk.

In the 1880s, the New York Central Hudson River Railroad did not own milk cars suitable to operate with high-speed trains, Thus the ND&CRR

transferred its milk cargo at Dutchess Junction to steamships for transportation to New York City. However, an older style of milk car did run on the NY&HRR, so the ND&CRR connected its milk cars to that railroad for shipment into New York City. In the 1890s, milk shippers and dealers pressured railroad lines to use "refrigerator cars." These cars did not have the refrigeration as they have today. The cars were insolated so as to prevent the ice from melting and to keep the milk cold. By then, the NYC&HRRR ran four such cars daily between Dutchess Junction and the city.

Coping with Bad Weather

Winter cold was probably the biggest challenge for the ND&CRR. Cold weather could freeze the Hudson River, stopping ferry movement across the river from Newburgh to Dutchess Junction and Fishkill Landing and thwarting the coal deliveries. In winter, the water in steam locomotives

Running through the Snow. Photograph from the Private Collection of J. W. Swanberg, Courtesy of J. W. Swanberg.

tended to freeze unless the tanks, pipes, and pumps were kept warm. If the fire to keep the pipes and pumps warm went out, they soon froze solid and were probably ruined.

Summer presented still another difficulty. If the days were dry, hot coal or smoldering wood belched from locomotive smokestacks, and sparks from railroad car wheels (trucks in railroad jargon) often started grass fires alongside the tracks. Most railroad stations had slate roofs to ward off the partially burned wood and coal flying through the air as the train passed. The Hopewell Junction depot sported such a roof. The Hopewell Junction Fire Department worked twenty-four/seven putting out fires either in the grass or up on the roof tops of buildings other than the station.

If not cold or heat, fog could be a challenge, too, as this *Letter Books* entry from December 9, 1892, illustrates, "In a heavy fog yesterday at about 4:30 near Tioronda trestle engine #7 struck one hand car which two section men were trying to get off the track. Both men were injured, and the hand car is a wreck" (volume 34, page 640).

Another weather predicament was wind. On Christmas Eve 1881, a strong wind blew an empty boxcar parked on a siding next to the Hopewell Junction water tank through the siding switch and out onto the main line. A locomotive hit the strayed boxcar head on, which damaged the locomotive. There is no record of what happened to the boxcar. Wind powerful enough to push a boxcar certainly could push over a telegraph—and later a telephone—pole, pulling down the vital lines of communication for the railroad as well as for the residents of the hamlets, towns, and villages the railroad ran through and stopped.

Most stations had a telegraph-telephone office. Messages from the main office of the ND&CRR would be sent out to a station located ahead of the train approaching the station. The telegraph-telephone operator took down the message and gave it to the conductor when the train arrived at the station. If the train was not scheduled to stop at the station, the operator tied the message to a huge hoop and waited outside for the train to pass by. The operator held the hoop high enough for a fireman or brakeman to lean out over the engine and to put his arm through the hoop, tear off the message, and fling the hoop who knew where along the track. The operator ran to find the hoop and then returned to the station (Levinson 5).

The Lighter Side of Railroading

Certain railroading events can only be classified as entertaining. In their time, many of these events were annoying, serious, and traumatic for those unfortunately involved. Yet, when viewed from the detached distance of our time, these events amuse many of us. The *Letter Books* inform us of several such incidents, some on the ND&CRR and others on the NY&NERR. Kimball wrote a letter to C. N. Chevalier, the superintendent of the NY&NERR on July 10, 1890, informing him:

> Wm. Carroll of Mattawan, NY & hat manufacturer [wrote a letter to us that] complains of the damage done to straw hats and stock by sparks and coals from your engines and especially engine 40. Will you please give the matter your attention and have the matter remedied as soon as possible. (Volume 30, page 25)

A farmer complained that train crews were stopping and stealing (eating?) apples from his orchard. A shipment of beer destined for Hopewell Junction arrived with half-empty bottles and the corks stuffed back in the necks. Shipments of boots and shoes not strapped shut went missing. Bells and lights attached to bicycles at departure points often were discovered detached at arrival points.

On a hot summer July day, a shipment of a large bag of smoked meat arrived in an unrefrigerated car at the ND&CRR station in Fishkill. The meat had been consigned to a butcher shop not in Fishkill but in Fishkill Landing (now Beacon). By the time the meat reached the Fishkill station, it smelled. The Fishkill station agent sent the meat down to the Fishkill Landing station. The station agent at Fishkill Landing sent for a local delivery wagon to carry the by now stinking load to the other end of Main Street where the butcher shop was located. However, the butcher refused the delivery. The delivery man took the bag of meat to a lard-rendering plant, left the bag at the plant, and beat a hasty retreat. All concerned in this reeking transaction, the shipper, the railroad, and the butcher, complained and demanded reparations. No record remains of apology and compensation. The delivery man stayed silent.

Chapter 4

Rivals of the Newburg, Dutchess, and Connecticut Railroad

The Poughkeepsie and Eastern Railroad

Thirty-four years after the DCRR received a charter issued by of New York State in 1832 to build a railroad from Poughkeepsie to the Connecticut state line, the Poughkeepsie and Eastern Railroad (P&ERR) received a state charter to build a railroad from Poughkeepsie to the Connecticut state line.

In *The Eagle's History of Poughkeepsie: From the Earliest Settlements, 1683 to 1905*, Edmund Platt explains the economic context for proposing the P&ERR:

> Most of the Harlem Valley ore was smelted in charcoal furnaces in the neighborhood and shipped to New York by the Harlem Railroad, but as wood began to grow scarcer an outlet to the Hudson River was sought, and in 1865 the mine owners built a piece of track about five miles long from the neighborhood of Boston Corners [in Columbia County] and announced that they would extend it [south] to Pine Plains [in Dutchess County], there to await the decision of the rival schemes for a river terminus. (214)

The motivation for the P&ERR was not the transportation of anthracite coal across Dutchess County. Instead, it was the acquisition of wood from barges, sloops, and steamships sailing on the Hudson River to be transported to charcoal furnaces in Columbia County.

The *Poughkeepsie Daily Eagle* began to agitate for the residents and entrepreneurs of Poughkeepsie to found, fund, build, and operate a railroad from the city east to the "country," as rural eastern Dutchess County was known to those living along the Hudson River. The agitation led to the state issuing a charter to the P&ERR. Within a month of receiving its charter, the company hired engineers to survey the road, prepared estimated construction costs, and offered stocks for sale. The publisher of the *Poughkeepsie Daily Eagle*, Isaac Platt, cheered on the P&ERR by telling the newspaper's readers that the stock sales would be successful (Mc Dermott 26).

The progress of the D&CRR, however, curbed the enthusiasm of the P&ERR and its cheerleading publisher. The D&CRR had completed its survey and began to grade its roadbed in mid-1867. Platt stated in the *Poughkeepsie Daily Eagle* that the completed D&CRR from Plum Point (later Dutchess Junction) would drain half of the trade business from

Building the Poughkeepsie and Eastern Railroad. Photograph from the Private Collection of J. W. Swanberg, Courtesy of J. W. Swanberg.

Poughkeepsie and severely depreciate property values (Friedrichsen 4). The publisher of the *Fishkill Standard*, John W. Spaight, countered Platt's predictions by stating that the D&CRR would benefit all the people and places in Dutchess County. Spaight acknowledged, though, that a railroad originating in Plum Point rather than in Poughkeepsie would be detrimental to Poughkeepsie's economy (Mc Dermott 26). Thus began the rivalry among many of the east-west, short-haul railroads and their originating communities in Dutchess County.

Despite Platt's predicted stock sales, the P&ERR had difficulty raising the funding for its line. The plan, broadly speaking, was to have the City of Poughkeepsie provide two-thirds of the money. The other third was to come from businessmen residing in Poughkeepsie; farmers whose lands lay along the railroad's route; and residents of the hamlets, towns, and villages through whose communities the railroad would run. Sales pitches were made to the businessmen, farmers, and residents. These pitches suggested increases in land values, population, and trade.

The pitches failed primarily because the farmers and the residents of the eastern communities believed that the D&CRR would be completed much sooner than the P&ERR. They anticipated the D&CRR trains transporting their goods, produce, and themselves to either the New York and Harlem or the Hudson River railroads and from there to Albany, New York City, or even Poughkeepsie. With waning interest east of the City of Poughkeepsie, businessmen in Poughkeepsie lost interest in the P&ERR, too (Mc Dermott 27).

Eventually, from June 1867 to March 1869, the taxpayers of the City of Poughkeepsie and of the various hamlets, towns, and villages along the proposed route of the P&ERR, including Ancram, Clinton, Pleasant Valley, and Stanford, voted to float bonds to fund the late-starting railroad, which was by then far behind the D&CRR.

By March 1869, building of the P&ERR resumed: rights-of-way were secured; grading of the road on the rights-of-way began; and gravel, ties, and rails arrived to be installed. Poughkeepsie's chief railroad yard was established on Smith Street on the western end of the P&ERR. A freight station, a passenger station, a turntable for locomotives, and a repair shop were built (Friedrichsen 4). The border hamlets, towns, and villages in both Dutchess County and Litchfield County, Connecticut, looked forward to shoppers and traders from across state lines traveling to their communities by the new train line rather than by horse and wagon. The eastern communities angled to change the direction of the railroad to pass through their neighborhoods using promised thousands of dollars as bait to the P&ERR. The route was not changed (Mc Dermott 36).

William Mc Dermott describes the inaugural run of a train on the P&ERR:

> On January 24, 1871, a celebration party with a band playing "Hail Columbia" preceded the P&E's first official trip. At 9:55 AM on that cold and stormy morning Engineer E. B. Cash and Fireman Robert Lester piloted "3 box cars fitted with seats and flooring covered with straw, one platform car and two new and elegant cars" all decked out with flags and banners left on a non-stop trip to Stissing. (35–36)

This account is reminiscent of the cheerful first run of a train on the ERR into Newburgh and on the BH&ERR from Dutchess Junction to Millbrook. New railroads approaching small towns and cities were events to be celebrated by the railroads and the residents of the communities, especially in mid-to-late nineteenth-century Dutchess County.

But the P&ERR did not deliver on many of its promises. Several of the dirt crossroads the railroad passed by never developed even into hamlets. Part of its anticipated revenue from transporting iron ore from mines located in Columbia County to furnaces located in Poughkeepsie never grew to the projected profits. The same was true for milk transported from dairy farms in Columbia and Dutchess Counties to the New York and Harlem Valley Railroad (Mc Dermott 36).

Financial support dwindled due to a weak bond market. The railroad could not extend its line from Pine Plains to the Connecticut state line. The residents of the border hamlets, towns, and villages did not see the expected increase in shoppers and traders. Residents of Poughkeepsie voted to float another bond to supply money to the railroad to complete its line from Pine Plains to the Connecticut state line. It did so in October 1872 (Mc Dermott 36).

Old Operations under New Names

The new booster shot of money did little to relieve the P&ERR's financial pain. In 1874, the P&ERR went into receivership and was sold in April 1875 to George Pelton of Poughkeepsie, who reorganized it and optimistically renamed it as the Poughkeepsie, Hartford, and Boston Railroad (PH&BRR). This new old railroad began operating on the same tracks with the same rolling stock and the same Poughkeepsie headquarters as the earlier line. The PH&BRR, however, never reached Hartford or Boston, but it did extend to Boston Corners in Columbia County. The PH&BRR lasted nine years, until 1884, when it, too, failed and went into receivership. Three years later, in 1887, it was sold, reorganized, and optimistically renamed the New York and Massachusetts Railway (NY&MRR). The NY&MRR made it for six years until 1893 when it, too, failed and was foreclosed. That same year it was sold, reorganized, and optimistically renamed the Poughkeepsie and Eastern Railroad Company (P&ERR). Five years later, in 1898, it failed and went into receivership until 1907, when it was sold to the New York, New Haven, and Hartford Railroad (NYNH&HRR), which immediately merged it with its supplementary, subordinate company the CNERR. History repeated itself—again and again and again.

William Mc Dermott delivers a dismal postmortem on the late P&ERR:

> Difficulty raising construction money and with no direct connection to the Hudson River and with no direct link to a railroad connected with the west, its chances for financial success were severely hampered from the start. Added to these was its failure to construct its own direct line to Millerton (State Line)—it had to lease the D&C track from Stissing Junction to Pine Plains. For all practical purposes it was hardly more than a short line through the towns of Poughkeepsie, Pleasant Valley, and a sliver of the town of Clinton, the only towns along its line where it did not compete with the D&C. Even at its point of origin, Poughkeepsie, it competed with freight revenue with the Hudson River Railroad. (36)

Dieter Friedrichsen describes a labor dispute that occurred before the P&ERR even completed constructing its line:

> In July 1869, the progress of the work was seriously interrupted. Walter Welch, subcontractor, financial comptroller, and [Poughkeepsie resident] swindled the men in his employ and various persons in the city and country out of more than $20,000.00 [$410,948.73 in 2021 money] and then disappeared. Not receiving their pay, the Irish workers threatened to destroy the grading and stone work (*sic*) they had done near Pleasant Valley. They cooled down before initiating their threat when it became known that Col. Smithfield of Pine Plains, one of Welch's associates, also disappeared. Despite Sheriff Kenworthy's best efforts, the laborers' revolt went into high gear and one of them, Jack McDonald, seized a horse and wagon, belonging to Welch, and refused to give it up. Company D of the 21st Regiment, under the command of Capt. William Haubennestel, was called in to Poughkeepsie to quell the riot and restore order. The property was recovered, and McDonald and others were arrested. It was never established whether the payroll was ever recovered. (5)

The workers' crime appears to have been interrupting the track work and seizing a horse and wagon. The justice meted out was the arrest of the aggrieved strikers. The disappearance of the contractors and the payroll appears as if it was beside the point. Christian Wolmar points out that as early as during the Civil War, "[t]he withdrawal of labor was a powerful weapon, and threats to strike were seen almost as a declaration of war. Strikes represented a real threat for companies with enormous, fixed assets on which they needed to obtain a return to satisfy shareholders" (231). If the P&ERR was not built, all the bonds floated by the residents of Poughkeepsie and the other hamlets, towns, and villages would not return any profit at all. The strike had to be suppressed, by the military, if necessary, if money was to be made.

An Iron Horse, an Iron Trail, and an Iron Mine: The Clove Branch Railroad

New York State issued a charter in 1868 to a short, four-mile railroad, the Clove Branch Railroad (CBRR). The next year, the CBRR began operation. During that same year, the D&CRR built tracks from Plum Point (later Dutchess Junction) through "New" Hopewell to Millbrook. The CBRR connected with the D&CRR just northeast of "New" Hopewell near where County Route 82 intersects the CBRR today.

The CBRR was essentially a spur of the D&CRR. However, the CBRR was chartered and operated as a separate railroad that reported to the D&CRR management as a supplementary, subordinate company. When the D&CRR went bankrupt and the ND&CRR began operation in 1877, it assumed management of the CBRR. Twenty years later, in 1897, the CBRR was abandoned, and the ND&CRR claimed its assets.

In 1877, the ND&CRR extended the CBRR from Sylvan Lake, where the iron mine was located, four miles east to Clove Valley. This extension enabled the CBRR to reach an iron furnace as well as a few more freight customers and passengers. Passenger traffic was light, and, eventually in March 1884, the Beekman Station on the CBRR was designated a flag stop for those few who wanted to ride the CBRR to the Clove Branch station and then connect with the ND&CRR trains for points north or south in Dutchess County.

Freight traffic was also light and consisted of mail and items addressed to factories and mills along the way to the iron mine and the iron furnace. The main source of revenue for the CBRR was iron ore, and when demand for that commodity slowed, the railroad's revenue barely covered its expenses. Starting in September 1887, some of the iron ore mined from Sylvan Lake was shipped not to the furnace at Clove Valley but to the furnace at Copake, New York. This convoluted but necessary means of transport just barely helped the CBRR's revenue crisis.

In addition to iron ore, the CBRR hauled charcoal to fire the iron furnace at Clove Valley. The charcoal was loaded into specially built wooden cars that were bulky but lightweight. These cars tended to catch fire because when the charcoal was loaded into the cars, it was still warm and even smoldering. A load of charcoal arrived at Clove Valley in February 1884 from Bennington, Vermont. On the way, one of the charcoal cars burned down to the rails, leaving only the car's hot trucks (wheels) and frame behind.

During the 1880s and 1890s, the CBRR hardly survived. Notes in the ND&CRR *Letter Books* refer to cutting operation expenses, reducing the labor force, salvaging some used track and switches from CBRR sidings for use on the ND&CRR tracks, and deferring repairs. Gradually, the CBRR was discontinued. The small iron mines, such as the one at Sylvan Lake, and the small iron furnaces, such as the one at Clove Valley, were losing the competitive battle with the huge, new iron mining operations in the Great Lakes region. Revenue losses for the CBRR grew larger. Mail delivery ceased in July 1891. Despite the cutbacks, a new fifty-foot steel bridge was delivered to and installed on the CBRR track in December 1891. The CBRR continued passenger traffic, including pleasure excursions to the grove at Sylvan Lake. On August 17, 1892, the Fishkill Methodist Sunday School class rode the train to Sylvan Lake.

The problems for the CBRR continued. The New York State Board of Railroad Commissioners required elm trees at Clove Branch Junction be removed, yet residents objected to the railroad removing the trees. The residents declared the trees stood as landmarks for deeds to local farms and shaded local homes; one resident threatened violence if trees in front of his house were felled.

The Tower brothers owned the Sylvan Lake iron mine and an iron furnace in Poughkeepsie. In April 1896, they notified the ND&CRR that they planned to close their iron furnace and that they would not need any more iron ore from the mine.

A Live Horse, a Dirt Trail, and an Iron Mine: The Clove Branch "Railroad"

On June 29, 1896, the ND&CRR applied to the New York State Board of Railroad Commissioners to close the CBRR (*Letter Books*, volume 42, page 430). On July 14, 1896, G. Hunter Brown wrote to the station agent at Sylvan Lake, C. W. Bryant, and to the station agent at Clove Branch

Junction, E. I. Miller. Brown was the new superintendent of the ND&CRR. He succeeded Charles Kimball when Kimball died in 1895 and was the son of George H. Brown, a founder of the D&CRR. Brown stated to the station agents:

> Please take notice that on or after August 1st, 1896 the Clove Branch Railroad will cease to be operated as the Clove Branch Railroad. [. . .] Please state to all concerned that the management of this Company regret exceedingly to be forced to take these necessary steps and sever the connections of themselves with the company, but as they themselves are aware the business of the Clove Branch Railroad has been nil for many months, and it hardly seems fair that the ND&C Co. should be obliged to pay all the expenses of the maintenance of this property without receiving any benefits from it. [. . .], Personally, if there is anything I can do to aid yourself and others in obtaining other situations, by means of letters of recommendation or otherwise issued from this office, I should be glad to do so. (Volume 43, page 62, 14 July 1896)

The letter appears a sudden and depressing abandonment of the CBRR and an insipid, kindly dismissal of the employees of a going-out-of-business railroad.

Between July 14 and August 1, 1896, excursion traffic dwindled to one trip by a Poughkeepsie Baptist Church group on July 20. Passenger ticket sales stopped after July 31. Freight deliveries occurred only on Saturdays. In October 1897, the Board of Directors of the ND&CRR voted to cease operation of the CBRR on December 31, 1897. Superintendent Brown wrote a letter to the eighteen customers in Beekman, Clove Valley, Gardiner Hollow, and Poughkeepsie announcing the end of the railroad—unless business increased dramatically. On December 29, 1897, the ND&CRR claimed all rolling stock of the CBRR in payment of debt owed to the ND&CRR by the CBRR. On January 15, 1898, the last weekly Saturday revenue train ran on the CBRR.

By the end of November, the tracks were gone. The CBRR was the first east-west, short-haul railroad in Dutchess County to have its rails taken up and its roadbed abandoned. On January 31, 1899, the New York State Board of Railroad Commissioners designated the Clove Branch Junction station a flag stop only; most trains would not even have to slow down for that station.

But this last dismissal of the CBRR was not the end of its story. Less than six months after taking up the rails of the CBRR, the management of the ND&CRR contemplated rebuilding the track because it wanted the iron-ore shipment revenues again. However, the land on which the original rails lay had reverted to the previous landowners who did not want a railroad running through their pastures and yards and who again refused to have their elm trees cut down.

Undaunted, the management of the ND&CRR imagined hauling the iron ore out of the mine at Sylvan Lake using horse-and-wagon teams or constructing another set of tracks that circumnavigated the landowners' property. Eventually, in June 1899, horse-and-wagon teams hauled the iron ore from the mine over a dirt road to the former Clove Branch Junction, a distance of four miles. Teamsters loaded the ore onto the low-sided gondolas of the ND&CRR. The ND&CRR transported the ore to Stissing Junction where it was turned over to the Poughkeepsie and Eastern Railroad Company (P&ERRC). This railroad transported the ore through Pleasant Valley to Poughkeepsie and delivered it to an iron furnace there.

Wanting to play a larger role in the transportation of iron ore from the Sylvan Lake mine and reap larger revenue, the ND&CRR built a new siding at Clove Branch Junction. Now the wagonloads of iron ore would be piled into the gondolas parked on the siding. Business from the mine boomed, so the ND&CRR ordered more gondolas. The railroad transported this new ore not to Stissing Junction but to Dutchess Junction. There it transferred the gondolas to the New York Central Railroad (NYCRR) for transportation to New York City and to Poughkeepsie.

With more gondolas, the ND&CRR demanded more wagon loads of ore. Gondolas were filled with as much as 46,000 pounds. *Letter Book* memos record a proposal to rebuild the CBRR rails once again to Sylvan Lake. Then for an unstated, sudden reason, the ore shipments halted more than a year after it was started; next, according to the *Letter Books*, it resumed on November 17, 1900; after October 1902, there is no more mention in the *Letter Books* of the CBRR, the iron-ore business, or rebuilding new tracks. To today's readers of the *Letter Books*, the mine seems to have faded away as did the railroad without fanfare or formal ending. It appears as far as the ND&CRR was concerned, that was the last of the CBRR.

On today's road maps, one can find Clove Branch, Sylvan Lake, Beekman, and Clove Valley, but these places are residential communities easily reached by vehicle over macadam roads. Sylvan Lake is a popular spot for summer camps, as it was when the CBRR shuttled parties from Poughkeepsie and Fishkill to the lake for daily outings. Over a hundred years of underbrush and trees obscure all traces of the railroad bed. The Beekman Golf Course covers part of the railroad's right of way. The Clove Valley Iron Furnace located on Furnace Road in Clove Valley stands in ruins. Like the railroad itself, the railroad stations at the Clove Branch Junction, Sylvan Lake, Beekman, and Clove Valley vanished.

The Northern Dutchess Alternative Coal Train: The Rhinebeck and Connecticut Railroad

New York State issued a charter in June 1870 to the Rhinebeck and Connecticut Railroad (R&CRR) to build a road from Rhinecliff to the Connecticut state line. Thomas Cornell, president of the Cornell Steamboat Company, mainly founded, funded, built, and operated the R&CRR himself. Cornell imagined a boat-train network that would transport anthracite coal from Kingston across the Hudson River to Rhinecliff. The coal would be unloaded from the Delaware and Hudson Canal boats onto his steamboats, ferried across the Hudson to Rhinecliff, unloaded from his steamboats into his railroad cars, and transported to Connecticut (Mc Dermott 37).

The logic behind his plan was two-fold. First, the canal boats of the Delaware and Hudson would travel a much shorter distance from Kingston to Rhinecliff than they traveled from Kingston to Dutchess Junction where they met the D&CRR. Second, the trains of the R&CRR would travel a shorter distance from Rhinecliff to the Connecticut state line than the D&CRR traveled from Plum Point (later Dutchess Junction) to the Connecticut state line.

Cornell imagined a route east through Pine Plains to the Connecticut state line. However, the actual route changed to the north through Red Hook and Mt. Ross (a hamlet of the Town of Pine Plains) in Dutchess County and Boston Corners in Columbia County before reaching the state line. The alternate route allowed the R&CRR to benefit from additional businesses in the larger towns and villages located in southern Columbia County, up until that time railroad-less (Mc Dermott 37).

In addition to anticipated freight and passenger traffic from northern Dutchess County and southern Columbia County, Cornell expected the residents of the towns and villages through which he planned his railroad to run to assist in funding the railroad. Rhinebeck and Milan residents agreed. The residents of other communities did not agree. Residents in Dutchess County opposed funding because they wished not to be "compulsory stockholders." Residents in Columbia County had already funded the P&ERR and thought funding a second railroad was too much (Mc Dermott 38). The balance of the funding came from private entrepreneurs.

In 1872, construction of the railroad began. In May, tracks were laid from Rhinecliff up the steep hill to Elizaville. The first passenger revenue runs began on July 4 from Elizaville to Rhinebeck to celebrate Independence Day. By spring 1874, the R&CRR was transporting calves, hay, and straw from the farms to the steamboats and barges at Rhinecliff and from there to New York City (Mc Dermott 39). Business was successful. In 1874, new locomotives and other cars were bought. The track was now constructed all the way through to the Connecticut state line.

Anthracite coal was transported by the R&CRR from Rhinecliff to Hartford, Connecticut. Cornell began charging one dollar more per ton of coal than he had previously charged to transport the coal. This increase in price made the cost of coal in his yard more than any other along the Hudson River. Unhappy with Cornell's fee, Rhinebeck residents contracted to have coal shipped from a coal yard in Newburgh up to Rhinebeck for delivery. Cornell retaliated by sabotaging the Newburg barges. For his disruption and damage to the barges, Cornell was arrested, tried, found guilty—but paid a trifling fine and nothing more (Mc Dermott 40).

Although business continued, the R&CRR began running a deficit. For the next five years, it yielded slim profits or large losses. In 1882, Cornell bought the failing railroad from its stockholders at a fraction of the cost it took to build it. He immediately sold it to the Hartford and Connecticut Western Railroad (H&CWRR) at a great personal profit. The R&CRR ceased to exist as an independent railroad and became a western extension of and a direct route to the Hudson River for the H&CWRR (McDermott 40).

Lyndon A. Haight observes that "[t]hese roads [the P&ERR, the Poughkeepsie and Connecticut (P&CRR), the CBRR, and the R&CRR] were family railroads, employing local people—fathers, sons, and daughters—who made their homes and paid taxes in Pine Planes and the neighboring towns of Dutchess and Columbia Counties" (29). When one of these several east-west, short-haul railroads failed, the families were in danger of failing, too. Often, another railroad, small or large, temporarily assumed ownership and operation of the failed one and continued to employ the family members and to save them temporality from collapse—until that small railroad failed, too or that large railroad sold its equipment or abandoned its buildings and laid off its employees.

The Short, Imagined Life of the New York, Boston, and Montreal Railroad

In 1872, while president of the D&CRR, George H. Brown entertained a still grander dream. He became president of another company, the New York, Boston, and Northern Railroad (NYB&NRR) and intended to connect several small railroads together to run trains from New York City to northern New York State. In January 1873, he extended the scope of his dream to include Montreal, Canada. So, Brown resigned as president of the NYB&NRR; dissolved the company; created a new company, the New York, Boston, and Montreal Railroad (NYB&MRR); and accepted its presidency. He planned to build a few short-link railroads to connect existing lines into a complete route from New York City to Montreal via Rutland, Vermont. The short-haul, east-west railroads, the D&CRR and the CBRR, were to be included as segments in this proposed long-haul, north-south railroad. Among the planned new short links were tracks from Brewster, New York, to the CBRR and from Pine Plains, New York, to Chatham, New York.

These imagined links were never built. The Financial Panic of 1873 not only dissolved Brown's dream of a Canadian American railroad empire but also sent the D&CRR into foreclosure. The proposed NYB&MRR vanished along with Brown's presidency of it. However, one imagined link eventually became the actual extension of the CBRR from Sylvan Lake to the iron furnace at Clove Valley. What real equipment the wished-for NYB&MRR owned was divided up among the existing east-west, short-haul railroads or sold to the highest bidder.

Twelve years later, in 1885, the *Letter Books of the Newburgh, Dutchess, and Connecticut Railroad* contain a retrospection of the events following the failure of the NYB&MRR. Superintendent Charles Kimball wrote a long letter to the president of the ND&CRR, John L. Schultze, detailing the disposition of the NYB&MRR property. Kimball concludes his letter with this reasonable observation and disclaimer, "All my records of this property having been destroyed by fire in April 1876, all the records I have, is a book, copied from another book then in Mr. J. Q. Hoyts office by Mr. J. E. Ralph, in 1876 after the fire. I presume this book is correct, but I could not attest to its [*sic*] correctness" (Volume 21, pages 241–43, 1 December 1885).

Kimball states what we all believe: that our remaining sources of information, such as the *Letter Books* and contemporary newspaper articles, are correct, but we cannot always confirm and, thereby, certify their truth and appropriateness.

Parallel Lines That Actually Converged: The New York and Massachusetts and The Poughkeepsie and Connecticut Railroads

When the Poughkeepsie-Highland Railroad Bridge opened in December 1888, the Poughkeepsie Bridge Company presumed the NY&MRR would connect the bridge with Connecticut. However, the owner of the NY&MRR, Henry D. Cone, refused to open his railroad to east-bound trains running over the bridge or to sell it to the Poughkeepsie Bridge Company (Mabee 57). The trains had nowhere to go once they crossed the bridge, so the Poughkeepsie Bridge Company built its own railroad. New York State issued a charter in 1887 to the company to build a railroad from Poughkeepsie to the Connecticut state line, the P&CRR (Mabee 57).

The P&CRR left Poughkeepsie right off the bridge and traveled northeast through Pleasant Valley and Pine Plains in Dutchess County, through Silver Nails in Columbia County, southeast on the Rhinebeck and Connecticut Railroad tracks to Canaan, Connecticut, and connected with the H&CWRR. The P&CRR and the NY&MRR ran parallel to each other and crossed over each other's tracks both near McIntyre and again near Salt Point. Along with the ND&CRR and the NY&MRR, the P&CRR was the third railroad to serve simultaneously Pine Plains (Haight 24–25).

The P&CRR was built from 1887 through 1889. In 1889, the P&CRR was merged with the H&CWRR into the CNERR, a subordinate, subsidiary railroad of the NYNH&HRR (Mabee 57). The brief existence of the P&CRR illustrates railroad surplus, excess, redundancy, and sudden extinction.

Chapter 5

The Birth of Hopewell Junction

An East-West, Long-Haul Railroad:
The New York and New England Railroad Reaches Hopewell

After the failure of the BH&ERR, its assets were reformed. The railroad emerged as the NY&NERR. It planned to build a ferry facility at Fishkill Landing (now Beacon), located about a mile north of the BH&ERR's intended site at Denning's Point and about two miles north of Dutchess Junction, the ferry facility of the ND&CRR.

To reach Fishkill Landing and to connect with the anthracite-coal ferries sailing across the Hudson River from Newburgh, the NY&NERR planned to construct a separate rail line from "New" Hopewell to the Hudson River. The line would have run parallel to the tracks constructed by the D&CRR in 1868 and now operated by the ND&CRR. However, the NY&NERR never built this redundant line, and instead, it bought rights on the existing ND&CRR tracks from "New" Hopewell to Wicopee, a location, not a community, located between the hamlets of Mattawan and Fishkill Landing, now combined into Beacon. At Wicopee, the NY&NERR then constructed its own track to Fishkill Landing.

Arrangements between the NY&NERR and the ND&CRR moved quickly over a seven-month period on five different fronts almost simultaneously.

In May 1881, the NY&NERR began constructing a line from "New" Hopewell to Danbury, Connecticut. The BH&ERR had previously completed the grading for tracks from "New" Hopewell to Danbury but laid little track. The section of track completed by the BH&ERR was the spur track on which George Brown marooned BH&ERR engines and cars in 1870 by pulling up some of the rails.

The major obstacle to laying the track from "New" Hopewell to Danbury was Whaley Lake, located in the Town of Pawling in southeastern Dutchess County. There was not enough room between the lake and the rocky hills next to it to build a track. The railroad elected to cross a part of the lake. As workers drove pilings into the lake bottom to support a bridge, they discovered the bottom of the lake was deep and partly filled with peat. After driving pilings more than 110 feet into the peat, the railroad settled on landfill. However, the fill promptly sank out of sight, so they added more fill, but peat began to rise up alongside the construction. Faced with a tight schedule, an uncooperative lake bottom, and no remaining options, the workers continued to add train loads of fill through the summer of 1881. They dumped eighty-thousand cubic yards of fill before the man-made ground finally stabilized. Then the landfill was constant enough to support a bed; ballast; ties; rails; and most of all a locomotive, a tender, and cars.

Next, in October, the NY&NERR ran a train from Hopewell to Wicopee over the ND&CRR's track. This train hauled gravel for laying the track bed from Wicopee to Fishkill Landing. To obtain more gravel, the ND&CRR gave permission to the NY&NERR to install a switch between the Fishkill and Glenham stations to access the ND&CRR's gravel pit.

A note dated October 8 states that a frog (railroad jargon for a switch) connecting the main line of the ND&CRR and the main line of the NY&NERR was ready to be installed October 17. The frog was installed December 8, 1881. On that date Hopewell became a junction.

Finally, between Wicopee Junction and Fishkill Landing, the NY&NERR encountered a second major obstacle. Its tracks had to cross the NYC&HRRR. Instead of installing a series of switches by which to cross onto and then over the NYC&HRRR as the D&CRR and now the ND&CRR did, the NY&NERR simply built a bridge. The bridge avoided all traffic conflicts between the two railroads. This simple solution was the same as the trestle built by the NY&NERR over the NY&HRR crossing (Turner 96–97). After crossing the NYC&HRRR, the tracks of the

NY&NERR curved north along the Hudson River toward Fishkill Landing, the ferry docks, and eventually the ferries themselves soon laden with anthracite coal. That track and the bridge are there today.

Fishkill Landing consisted of a long stretch of pilings driven into the east bank of the Hudson River to support sets of tracks. At the river end of the tracks, the ferries docked, coal cars aboard the ferry were connected to a backed-up locomotive and tender, and the locomotive pulled the cars out of the ferry and onto dry land consisting of a considerable amount of fill between the river and the NYC&HRRR tracks. Once under way, the coal train left Fishkill Landing, crossed over the bridge, headed first to the switch at Wicopee Junction, then east to Hopewell Junction, and eventually southeast to Danbury, Connecticut, and points east. This spliced route continued until 1904.

One of the first NY&NERR trains to leave Fishkill Landing contained not coal but live turkeys from Livonia, New York, a town south of Rochester. The turkeys were bound for Christmas dinner tables in Boston (McDermott 41). This produce and its destination illustrate the major difference between the NY&NERR and the several east-west, short-haul railroads operating in Dutchess County. The former railroad was not interested in produce from Dutchess County but from western New York State and beyond. It was not interested in transporting that produce to Albany or New York City but across three state lines to Boston. In this way, the NY&NERR resembled the long-haul NY&HRR and the NYC&HRRR more than it resembled the short-haul Dutchess County railroads.

High over the Hudson: The Poughkeepsie-Highland Railroad Bridge

Carlton Mabee wrote a history of the founding, funding, building, and operation of the Poughkeepsie-Highland Bridge, *Bridging the Hudson: The Poughkeepsie Railroad Bridge and Its Connecting Lines*. For this reason, we will confine our discussion on the positive impact the bridge made on the transportation of coal and other freight into and through Dutchess County and on the negative impact it had on the east-west, short-haul railroads running in Dutchess County.

By early 1890, the ND&CRR, the New NY&NERR, the R&CRR, and the PH&BRR felt the competition from the Poughkeepsie-Highland Bridge. Trains on the bridge route transported the coal much faster and more efficiently than the ferry-car routes. On the bridge route, intact coal trains left Campbell Hall and, later, from 1904 on, Maybrook, both huge rail yards in Orange County. These trains ran over the bridge and headed east on the P&CRR into central New England and later southeast on the DCRR into southern New England.

On the ferry-car route, ERR coal cars had to be loaded onto a ferry and uncoupled from the locomotives at Newburgh, sailed across the Hudson River to Dutchess Junction or Fishkill Landing, and recoupled to locomotives there. On the Delaware and Hudson Canal barge route, the coal on the barges was reloaded into ferries, sailed across the Hudson to Rhinecliff, and reloaded once again into the cars of the R&CRR. Whether by ferry from Newburgh or by barge from Kingston to Dutchess Junction, Fishkill Landing, Poughkeepsie, or Rhinecliff, the speed of the delivery of anthracite coal stopped when the Hudson River froze in winter, just when the coal was needed most.

Dutchess Junction, Fishkill Landing, and the coal docks at Poughkeepsie and Rhinecliff continued to compete with the bridge and with each other for coal business from 1888 to 1904, but the struggle between the railroad bridge and the railroad ferries was a losing battle. Bickering between the ND&CRR and the bridge route erupted when "the Bridge Route's General Freight Agent [. . .] accused the ND&CRR of deliberately intending to "jab" the Bridge Route, while the ND&CRR's General Freight Agent [. . .] accused the Bridge Route of not adhering to its published rates, but instead doing 'vicious' secret rate cutting to favor certain customers" (Mabee 129). How—or if—this quarrel of "jabs" and "vicious rates" was resolved is unknown. By 1904, the bridge route siphoned off enough traffic from the ferry-car service to compel the NYNH&HRR, by then the owners of Fishkill Landing, to close the ferry docks.

When the Poughkeepsie-Highland Bridge opened, the *Poughkeepsie Eagle* gave an account of the first train to venture out onto the bridge. Carlton Mabee paraphrased the account in this way:

> Starting from Poughkeepsie, the train moved slowly at first. As it passed along Parker Avenue, track workers dropped

Poughkeepsie-Highland Bridge, c. 1904. Photograph by Detroit Publishing Co., Prints and Photograph Collection, Library of Congress.

their tools, and climbed onto the train wherever they could. [. . .] As the train moved onto the bridge's approach viaduct, [Pomeroy P.] Dickinson [the Poughkeepsie Bridge Company's engineer] tootled his whistle, passengers in the train waved their handkerchiefs, onlookers gawked. When the train crossed high over the New York Central's Hudson Line tracks locomotives below shrieked forth an enthusiastic salute. Then, as many people on both sides of the river marveled to see, the train rumbled at a lively rate out over the Hudson. When Dickenson decided the train was not shaking the bridge, not even giving it a tremor, it was probably the proudest moment of his life. (53–54)

Today, cyclists, joggers, runners, and walkers who enter from the Poughkeepsie side of the Walkway over the Hudson clearly follow the initial train's passage from Parker Avenue, across the viaduct, to the center of the bridge, and on to the other side. The Walkway over the Hudson is the former Poughkeepsie-Highland Railroad Bridge refurbished and resurfaced with concrete and is now a New York State Park.

The Last East-West, Short-Haul Railroad: The Dutchess County

In 1886, more than two years before the construction of the Poughkeepsie-Highland Railroad Bridge was completed, the New York State issued a charter to the Poughkeepsie and South Eastern Railroad (P&SERR). The P&SERR planned to build a line from Poughkeepsie southeast through LaGrange, Wappinger, and East Fishkill, to the hamlet of Hopewell Junction. There the line would connect with the NY&NERR. In this way, the line would connect the Poughkeepsie-Highland Bridge with southern Connecticut and Rhode Island as the P&CRR connected the bridge with Hartford, Connecticut, and Boston, Massachusetts, thus expanding the Poughkeepsie Bridge Company's commercial interests.

In 1889, construction of the line began—then stopped. A year later, the reorganized and refinanced P&SERR, now known as the Dutchess County Railroad (DCRR) picked up the construction and followed a similar plan as the former railroad. The rail route the DCRR constructed is essentially the route of the William R. Steinhaus Dutchess Rail Trail from Hopewell Junction to the Walkway over the Hudson in Poughkeepsie that cyclists, joggers, runners, and walkers follow today. The construction of the DCRR concerned the ND&CRR and the NY&NERR. To the two railroads already running through Hopewell Junction, a third railroad running through the hamlet made a troublesome crowd.

According to the *Letter Books*, in 1890, the DCRR intended to connect with the NY&NERR east of where the Hopewell Junction depot was located at the intersection of Railroad Avenue and Bridge and Center Streets. By connecting with the NY&NERR, the DCRR would be favorably positioned to build a direct line parallel to the ND&CRR Clove Branch line all the way to the Clove Valley iron-ore furnace. The DCRR intended to negotiate an arrangement with the owners of the furnace to transport the iron north to Poughkeepsie and west across the Poughkeepsie-Highland Bridge.

This proposed arrangement alarmed the ND&CRR, which wanted to keep the iron traffic for itself. The ND&CRR told the DCRR to connect with the NY&NERR west of the depot, thus making the building of any line from Hopewell Junction to Clove Valley difficult for the DCRR.

DUTCHESS COUNTY R R
READY FOR BUSINESS
Saturday, May 21, 1892.

On the above date the people on the line of the road and beyond are invited to participate in the festivities attending the opening of the line for business, consisting of an

EXCURSION TO POUGHKEEPSIE AND RETURN,
FREE OF CHARGE.

Train will leave Hopewell Junction at 10.50 A. M.; Fishkill Plains, 11.00 A. M.; Didell's, 11.17 A. M.; Manchester Bridge, 11.30 A. M., and upon reaching Poughkeepsie will proceed

OVER THE GREAT BRIDGE,

returning to Poughkeepsie at 12.00 o'clock.

Returning the train will leave Poughkeepsie at 4.30 P. M., arriving at Hopewell Junction in season to connect with trains on the New York & New England and Newburgh, Dutchess and Connecticut Railroads.

The **Board of Trade** and the **Retail Merchants' Association** of Poughkeepsie will be happy to welcome their friends from the interior of the county, who participate in the above excursion, and invite them to

A LUNCHEON,
At the New Armory on Market Street,
At 2.00 P. M.,

where there will be appropriate exercises, consisting of music and addresses by several gentlemen, etc.

I. W. FOWLER,	C. A. HAYES,
General Superintendent.	General Freight and Pass. Agent.

Hartford, Conn.

Announcement for the Dutchess County Railroad: "Ready for Business."

Eventually, the DCRR did connect with the NY&NERR east of the depot but did not build a line from Hopewell Junction to Clove Valley.

Tempests in a Teapot:
Railroad Contentions in Hopewell Junction

The junction of the NY&NERR and the ND&CRR proved difficult for the ND&CRR management. The two railroads differed, disagreed, and disliked each other. First, the NY&NERR operated 478 miles of track across four states, while the ND&CRR operated only fifty-eight miles of track across one county. Second, the much larger railroad company moved into the ND&CRR territory, building facilities on its own such as sidings at Hopewell Junction and the ferry docks at Fishkill Landing.

President John Schultze and general manager Charles Kimball of the ND&CRR had still other concerns about the relationship of their railroad and the NY&NERR. One concern involved the Hopewell Junction train yard. The NY&NERR wanted to change the alignment of the ND&CRR main line to make way for more sidings for the NY&NERR. Not surprisingly, the ND&CRR objected. The ND&CRR must have prevailed because maps and photographs of the train yard show the ND&CRR roadbed to have remained straight through Hopewell Junction.

Another concern entailed the demanding challenge of keeping trains, both passenger and freight, safe for both the ND&CRR and the NY&NERR. A sampling of letters from the *Letter Books* of the ND&CRR over a seven-week period illustrate the frustrations the two railroads encountered as they ran scheduled trains in both directions over one eleven-mile section of single track between Hopewell Junction and Wicopee Junction:

> December 13, 1881: Orders for the NY&NE gravel train to stay out of the way of other trains.

> December 14, 1881: Letter to the NY&NERR stating that no NY&NERR train will do local freight business between Hopewell Junction and Wicopee Junction.

December 14, 1881: Orders to the ND&CRR agent at Hopewell Junction to intercept any ND&CRR or Clove Branch cars that arrive on the NY&NERR from the east.

January 2, 1882: Letter to the NY&NERR division superintendent asking that extra trains be run during the day because the ND&CRR did not want to hire more switchmen for the night shift.

January 21, 1882: Letter to the NY&NERR complaining that their trains were going too fast when passing the Matteawan station crossing.

January 23, 1881: Letter to all agents stating that ND&CRR tickets were no longer valid on NY&NERR trains.

January 28, 1881: Letter reporting that a NY&NERR train struck the rear of ND&CRR train #4 at North Glenham Bridge after the colliding train made the run from Fishkill Landing (one and three-quarter miles away) in two minutes.

Reading just these seven communications from the *Letter Books*, one is aware of the ND&CRR's exasperation as it attempted to control scheduling between a local east-west, short-haul railroad and a multistate, east-west, long-haul railroad. This same conflicting relationship continued for over twenty years. From the point of view of the ND&CRR, safety trumped speed; from the point of view of the NY&NERR, speed trumped safety. The NY&NERR wanted to move freight as fast as possible for maximum profit and believed it was dealing with a slow-traffic bottleneck from Hopewell Junction to Wicopee Junction. The ND&CRR wanted to move freight and passengers as slowly and safely as possible as it had for the past four years and believed it was dealing with a reckless railroad pushing it off the track and out of the way.

The consolidation locomotives used by the NY&NERR dismayed the ND&CRR. These locomotives were built heavier and more powerful than those used by the ND&CRR. In June 1882, the ND&CRR complained to the NY&NERR that the consolidations ran at an unsafe speed of twenty-five to thirty miles per hour over the ND&CRR tracks. Then the ND&CRR requested that NY&NERR conductor Brigham and engineer Miller be suspended for running thirty-five miles per hour. The NY&NERR ignored the ND&CRR complaint and request. The excessive speed and weight of the consolidation-locomotive trains wore out the ND&CRR tracks and bridges and compelled the ND&CRR to repair and replace them. The ND&CRR banned the consolidation locomotives from running over the tracks and bridges until the work on the tracks and bridges was completed.

Wrecks created another issue between the ND&CRR and the NY&NERR. "The NERR (NY&NERR) had an eight-car wreck at Brinckerhoff (Town of Fishkill) yesterday. ND&C crew is working with the NE people, but the line will not be clear till Monday night" (volume 41, page 248, 21 March 1896).

The ND&CR and the NY&NER disagreed about the cause of the wreck. "NE said it was a defective switch point [therefore, the wreck was the ND&CRR's fault because that railroad maintained the track] and ND&C said it was a rotten car sill that broke [therefore, the wreck was the NY&NERR's fault because that railroad maintained the car]" (volume 41, pages 270–72, 26 March 1896). The argument was over who would pay for the cleanup.

The ND&CRR had issues with the DCRR, too. In addition to the DCRR's plot to build a branch line from Hopewell Junction to Clove Valley and butt in on the ND&CRR transportation of iron ore, nonpayment of bills was issue. ND&CRR superintendent Charles Kimball wrote ND&CRR president John Schutze that "DC RR has not paid for 2 months of flagman service at the Hopewell crossing. The flagman has been withdrawn and the DC RR warned about protection" (volume 33, pages 429, 430, 15 April 1892).

Because there was no flagman to protect the crossing at Hopewell, the NDCRR blocked the tracks, so no DCRR trains could cross. However, this action did not stop the DCRR crew. With DCRR officials on board a through train to sanction their efforts, a DCRR crew removed the pile of ND&CRR ties and reconnected the derail points. Then, posing as a NY&NERR train, the DCRR train crossed the ND&CRR tracks and proceeded on its way without ND&CRR permission.

Chapter 6

Changes to Hopewell Junction

An Assortment of Boardroom Mergers

In 1884, a little over three years after its arrival in Hopewell Junction, the NY&NERR fell behind in its mortgage payments and unfunded debt imbursements. The railroad's Board of Directors voted to place the company in receivership (Turner 103). Within the next year, the railroad's revenues improved, and enough of its debt was paid down for the it to be discharged from that receivership (Turner 105),

Yet being discharged from receivership was not a guarantee for running in the black to the NY&NERR. Its board considered renting its property to the NYNH&HRR to receive more income. Before it did, however, the president of the Philadelphia and Reading Railroad (P&RRR), Archibald Angus McLeod, took control of the stock of the NY&NERR. Like Cornelius Vanderbilt with the NY&HRR in the mid-1850s, McLeod's presence and power promised another way out of the NY&NERR's fiscal dilemma (Turner 117). But it proved not.

McLeod's colossal goal in 1892 included forming a new corporation, the Philadelphia, Redding, and New England Railroad Company (PR&NERRC). This blended company bought and merged with the former Poughkeepsie Bridge Company, now the Poughkeepsie Bridge Route, the P&CRR, and the DCRR all three operated then by the Central New England and Western Railroad (CNE&WRR) (Mabee 64). Now McLeod owned a through rail route from Pennsylvania to Connecticut. The NY&NERR nonetheless was not part of McLeod's massive merger.

In 1893, the NY&NERR filed for bankruptcy again. It applied for receivership again. For the next two years, creditors swarmed over the railroad, laying claim to its locomotives and cars. Two years later, the NY&NERR emerged out of receivership again and returned as the New England Railroad (NERR). Its president was the president of the NYNH&HRR (Turner 137).

The same year, 1895, J. Pierpont Morgan bought all the NERR stock and offered it all to the NYNH&HRR stockholders at cost (Turner 138). Thus, the NYNH&HRR controlled the NERR. The NYNH&HRR then relegated the management of the NERR to its subordinate, subsidiary the CNERR. Eventually, in 1927, the CNERR was absorbed into its parent company the NYNH&HRR. In the end of this merger era, the NYNH&HRR remained the last independent railroad.

The Development and Expansion of Hopewell Junction

William N. Anthony published and edited *The Hopewell Weekly News* from January 5, 1899, to December 13, 1900. During that brief time, the NYNH&HRR, through its subordinate, subsidiary railroad the CNERR, expanded its facilities at Hopewell Junction. The purpose of the expansion was to manage the increased train traffic coming through Hopewell Junction from the Poughkeepsie-Highland Bridge as well as the normal train traffic also coming through Hopewell Junction from Dutchess Junction to Millerton. Following are excerpts from the local newspaper chronicling firsthand and exercising cautious optimism about this development and expansion.

January 5, 1899

While the work of grading and laying of the tracks in the big yard of the [NYNH&HRR] lasts, [. . .] it may be of lasting benefit to the place. [. . .] To the casual observer, it looks like quite a gigantic piece of work, and that it may bring profitable results in the growth of our village, and to our business men [*sic*].

The boom Hopewell Junction is now enjoying came out of a sale by Mr. Lawrence C. Rapalje of land comprising about 25 acres to the NYNH&HRR to be used as a storage yard for freight cars.

The contract for grading was given to Messrs. Lathrop & Shea, of New Haven, the firm commencing the work about November 1st, soon after employing a force of about 150 men, 50 horses, carts, and wheel-scrapers, besides the construction train with the little engine "Maggie."

There are about 50 cars on the grounds; they are used in hauling earth. The working force has been reduced considerably during the past few weeks owing to the inability of the contractors to employ so many men and carts to good advantage.

The men and horses necessary for the carrying on of the work have been boarded on the grounds and by people in and out of the village, this being a source of revenue that comes acceptable in the winter season.

The construction of this big railroad yard naturally makes lively times in Hopewell Junction, and our merchants and others derive their share of the results of the improvement. The handling of so many cars here and the making up of trains when the yard is in full working order must necessarily make Hopewell Junction a more important railroad point than heretofore.

All this requires more help, and probably a number of railroad men and their families may locate here. It is thought that possibly the [NYNH&HRR] may erect repair shops and a round house at the new yard.

January 19, 1899

Lathrop & Shea, the contractors, have shut down work at the big railroad yard in Hopewell Junction owning to the fact that the cold weather has caused the ground to freeze so hard and solid that scarcely any progress could be made in excavating and grading. [. . .] The Italians and others employed in the work were discharged last Saturday, gangs of them leaving for New York that evening.

January 26, 1899

It is reported that a number of houses are to be built in Hopewell Junction in the Spring [sic]. Undoubtedly this report is true. That our village needs more dwellings and business places is an undeniable fact, and the sooner the work is commenced the better it will be. There is a healthy outlook for the growth of the village, and our citizens who have land and means will no doubt find it a good investment to build, at least a few houses. Everyone should take an interest in the general improvement. Make it a pleasant and healthful place of residence.

Hopewell Junction Rail Yard. Photograph collection of the late Ken Shuker.

March 30, 1899

Two fires last week in Hopewell has [sic] started considerable talk among the young men of the village to organizing a home fire department. There is hardly a doubt, but the required number of members could be obtained to man the machine [. . .]. A well-organized fire company is one of the first institutions a village needs when it becomes of any size beyond that of a little hamlet, and as Hopewell Junction has already advanced to quite a respectable sized town and bids fair to be much larger, why not have a fire department. At present [there] are no facilities to put out a fire.

May 25, 1899

Mr. Charles Underhill has completed a telephone line in Hopewell Junction which should prove a convenient service. The line connects the union depot with the telegraph station, also with the Central New England depot and Mr. Underhill's residence.

Geraniums, Coleuses, and other plants from Issac Vermilyea's conservatory are being placed in the flower beds on the north side of the railroad station. A month or two later and the beds will be very ornamental and attractive.

Rocked Forward and Rolled Backward: Relocating the Depot

From circa 1873 to 1905, the Hopewell Depot served exclusively first the D&CRR, the railroad that built it, and the ND&CRR, the railroad that maintained it. In 1881, the NY&NERR entered Hopewell, established it as a junction, and built its own small station. This building was located at Main Street underneath the present County Route 82 overpass that goes over the single remaining track in Hopewell Junction. In 1892, the DCRR arrived in Hopewell Junction and built its own passenger shelter where its track crossed the ND&CRR track and met the NY&NERR track. The location of both stations was not ideal for passengers who wished to switch lines to the ND&CRR. They had to walk several hundred yards through an active train yard or even longer through the streets of Hopewell Junction to reach the Hopewell Junction depot and the ND&CRR line at the corner of Railroad Avenue and Center and Bridge Streets.

To control the traffic of these three railroads so that it moved safely and timely through Hopewell Junction, a switch and a two-story signal tower was built by the ND&CRR circa 1892. The top floor of Signal Station #196 provided a commanding view of all the rail approaches into Hopewell Junction and was connected by telephone with the depot after 1899. Workers in the signal station operated several levers that controlled semaphores that indicated to train conductors and engineers on how to move through the junction. (A "semaphore" is a pole featuring either an arm attached to the pole or color lights fixed atop the pole that display their different indications either by altering the angle of the slant of the arm or by the selection of a different color.) With two trains running in opposite directions, the engineer of one of the trains may be indicated to move the train over to a siding and the engineer of the other train may be indicated to continue running through the junction.

To eliminate long, dangerous walks for passengers between the stations of the three railroads, in 1905, the CNERR, which by then operated all three of the railroads that ran through Hopewell Junction for the NYNH&HRR, moved the Hopewell Junction depot. The depot was pulled from its original location at the corner of Center and Bridge Streets and Railroad Avenue to beside the CNERR track and across the track from Signal Station #196. This track was now known as the Maybrook Line and ran from New Haven, Connecticut; through Danbury, Connecticut and Hopewell Junction; to the Poughkeepsie-Highland Railroad Bridge; and finally, to the rail yard in Maybrook, in Orange County. The depot remained alongside the track formerly owned by the ND&CRR and that ran from Dutchess Junction to Millerton.

Buildings were moved in the nineteenth and early twentieth centuries by horses or oxen and huge wooden poles, similar to telephone poles. The building was jacked up, the poles were slid under it, and the animals were harnessed to one end of it. The animals walked and pulled, and the poles

Hopewell Junction Depot, 1905. Photograph Courtesy of the East Fishkill Historical Society.

gradually rotated. When the back pole rolled out from under the building, the animals were halted, and the back pole was brought to the front of the building and placed under it. The animals resumed their plod, and the building slowly moved forward. The building made its destination. Thus, the depot was rolled from Center Street, along Railroad Avenue, alongside the former ND&CRR track to in front of the CNERR track.

In 1910, the CNERR, upgraded the Maybrook Line in anticipation of more east-west bridge traffic. It straightened curves on the track from Poughkeepsie to Danbury and built a second track from Poughkeepsie to Danbury. The building of this second track caused the CNERR to roll the Hopewell Junction depot back twenty-five to thirty feet to its present location and to add a half-cellar under its west end. A floor hatch and stairs to the cellar were added in the corridor between the two waiting rooms.

However, during this second move, the east-side chimney was lost. That event is not unusual given the jostling caused typically by the hauling animals and the ground over which the building traveled. In the restored depot today, part of a wall indicates where the missing chimney used to be. There exists no foundation under which the missing chimney would have been, so it is deduced the chimney was never rebuilt. Also, circa 1905, on or about the first move of the depot, the tops of three of the doors lost their basket-handle, rounded tops and were replaced by square tops. Round tops do not seal well, especially in winter, while square tops do, according to comments made in the *Letter Books*. Why the top of the fourth door kept its basket-handle, rounded shape is unknown.

The depot has remained in this location for 112 years. The DCRR passenger shed and the NY&NERR passenger station were torn down, the latter in 1935; two years after the NYNH&HRR suspended the passenger service of the ND&CRR in 1933.

The End of the Newburgh, Dutchess, and Connecticut Railroad

By 1892, nine different railroads made their separate ways through Dutchess County owned by eight different corporations. After 1892, the same railroads eventually became owned through an assortment of boardroom mergers by just one railroad: the NYNH&HRR. The NYNH&HRR was not interested in the whole line of the ND&CRR; it was interested in the ND&CRR section from Hopewell Junction through Wicopee Junction to Fishkill Landing. At Fishkill Landing (now Beacon), the NYNH&HRR wanted to connect with the NYC&HRRR. With this goal in mind, the NYNH&HRR began a series of abandonments. It discontinued ferry service and passenger service at Fishkill Landing in 1904 after it acquired the NY&NERR. The NYNH&HRR sold most of the buildings at Dutchess Junction for salvage in 1907. Freight and passenger service, however, continued from Dutchess Junction to Millerton on the ND&CRR, although it proved unprofitable for the NYNH&HRR.

The NYNH&HRR was mainly interested in an east-west freight service across the Poughkeepsie-Highland Railroad Bridge. After acquiring the NY&NERR from Danbury to Hopewell Junction and the DCRR from Hopewell Junction to the bridge, the NYNH&HRR had a direct route from Connecticut over the Hudson River to the rail yard at Maybrook. In 1910, the NYNH&HRR upgraded the Maybrook Line in anticipation of more east-west bridge traffic. It straightened curves on the track from Poughkeepsie to Danbury and built a second track from Poughkeepsie to Danbury.

With Dutchess Junction gone in 1907, the principal purpose of what had been Dutchess Junction shifted to Hopewell Junction. The junction yard was expanded to accommodate pusher steam engines. These engines were built large and powerful. They pushed from behind the caboose the heavy freight trains traveling from Hopewell Junction east to Danbury over Pawling Mountain, approximately 1,132 feet high. A water tower, a coal pocket, a repair shop, and a round table, were built to service these pusher engines. The repair shop serviced as many as thirty engines a day.

In 1916, the NYNH&HRR discontinued all train service on the ND&CRR from Dutchess Junction. The rails from Dutchess Junction to Wicopee Junction were pulled up, the switch was disconnected, and the Tioronda Bridge over the Fishkill Creek was sold for scrap. The NYC&HRRR continued to serve Dutchess Junction until about 1950 with a single, small building serving as the station.

The CNERR operated the ND&CRR from 1905 to 1927 when the CNERR was formally absorbed into the New Haven Railroad, The ND&CRR, of course, was absorbed into the NYNH&HRR, too. Passenger service on the ND&CRR from Hopewell Junction to Millerton continued until 1933.

Where All the Fares Went

Before the rails reached Dutchess County, turnpike roads adequately connected its communities for short-distance trading of goods and produce. Yet turnpikes inadequately connected its communities for long-distance trade, such as to Albany or New York City, because there were too many high-priced tolls to pay along the way. Thus, farmers and merchants chose to transport their produce and goods to Albany and New York City by steamboat, sloop, and barge sailing on the Hudson River. Travelers followed suit with the farmers.

The long-distance transportation of goods, produce, and people in the mid-Hudson Valley changed between 1848 and 1849, when the NY&HRR and the HRRR reached Dutchess County. Between the two railroads, the goods and produce of Dutchess County were transported to the New York City and Albany markets in larger bulks, by faster times, and through all seasons than the steamboats, sloops, and barges. The two railroads transported travelers to New York City and Albany faster, and in all seasons, too.

Not only in Dutchess County but also across the United States and its developing territories, the railroads trumped turnpikes and waterways from the 1850s up to the 1930s. Yet, one hundred years after Dutchess County farmers, merchants, and passengers forsook the roads first for boats and then for railroads, the roads returned to prominence at the expense of the rails.

The railroads influence on transporting freight and passengers waned in the 1930s. The railroads were undercut by the Great Depression from 1929 to 1939, by the improvement and expansion of paved roads, and by the automobiles and the trucks that rolled over them. The stock-market crash and the Great Depression that followed sent many of the companies that made the goods and produce transported by the trains into bankruptcy. Due to a lack of business, many railroads declared bankruptcy, too. More roads were paved. More cars and trucks were sold and were built to run farther. Car owners left when they wanted and arrived when they wanted. Truckers arrived at the farmer's barn and at the merchant's loading dock to pick up the produce and goods directly and transport them directly

Relocated Hopewell Junction Depot. A photograph by J. P. Ahrens in April 1934 showing on the near left the Hopewell Junction Depot and on the far left the Hopewell Junction Freight House; in the middle, the double tracks of the NYNH&HRR leading north to Poughkeepsie; and on right Signal Tower #196. Between the depot and the freight house is the single track of the old Newburgh, Dutchess, and Columbia Railroad running from Dutchess Junction to Millerton. Photograph from the Collection of J. W. Swanberg, Courtesy of J. W. Swanberg.

to their destinations. Truckers carried what goods and produce they preferred and charged the farmer and merchant what they chose (Wolmar 304-08). The Works Progress Administration provided many out-of-work men and women the opportunity to earn a living helping to build more paved roads (Wolmar 308).

One local result of this paved-road revolution was the cancelling of passenger service from Hopewell Junction to Millerton in 1933 and of freight service from Hopewell Junction to Millerton in the mid-1930s on the ND&CRR. With no traffic, the rails were pulled up from Hopewell Junction to Millerton by 1938. One of the reasons the ND&CRR ended its passenger and freight is evident in the photograph: automobiles and trucks. The track's abandonment signaled more than the outcome of the mergers of the nine railroads of Dutchess County and the end of the county's 19th-century experiment with east-west, short-haul railroads. It also signaled the diminishing importance of the Hopewell Junction Depot and of the hamlet that grew up around it.

The Abandoned Track of the ND&CRR. In the center of the frame is the abandoned track and beyond it the empty roadbed of the ND&CRR. The track was pulled up from Hopewell Junction to Millerton by 1938. To the left of the frame in the middle distance is the Hopewell Junction Freight House, and to the right of the frame and in the middle distance is the Hopewell Junction Depot. Beyond the depot is Signal Station #196 soon to be torn down. Photograph from the Collection of J. W. Swanberg, Courtesy of J. W. Swanberg.

Near the end of passenger service, the ND&CRR attempted to cut costs by switching from steam trains to gasoline-powered rail buses based on the adage that "if you can't beat 'em, join 'em." The rail buses had 60- to 120-horsepower engines and manual transmissions, like trucks. Their wheels were train wheels, or trucks in railroad jargon. These rail buses ran from Pine Plains to Beacon and from Copake through Pine Plains to Poughkeepsie daily. Some rural school children recalled to Bernard Ruberg riding the "Galloping Goose" to class in Beacon or Poughkeepsie. In 1933, the ND&CRR discontinued the rail buses along with the steam-train passenger service.

Rail Bus and Rail Bus with Two Drivers. Photographs from the Collection of J. W. Swanberg, Courtesy of J. W. Swanberg.

Chapter 7

Living in Hopewell Junction
1920s–1950s

Charlotte Dodge's Saunter around Hopewell Junction, 1923

Next to Stevens' [house on Route 82] was an orchard belonging to our farm which contained a few old apple trees, and those trees produced very early yellow apples. It was such a treat after the winter and summer drought of no fresh apples. These trees were also good for climbing.

Beyond the orchard was Coleman's Red Onion hotel and bar. "Red" because that was its color; "Onion" I know not why. The hotel burned in later years. The cause unknown but many fires were caused by cinders flying from the engines. It was a marvel of the times that Mrs. Coleman's diamond ring was found in the ashes.

As we approach the railroad tracks, we are stopped by Mr. Wensle who was the guardian of the tracks. He has come out of his little shed with his paddle with a "stop" sign showing; the opposite side reads "go," which he exhibits when the track is clear. Some days we would argue with this man, saying that we can beat that train.

Be it known, that if one was held up by one of these trains it could be a lengthy wait because there are many cars on the freights, sometimes numbering over a hundred, with an extra engine in the rear or several engines in the front to help pull or push the cargo over Pawling Mountain.

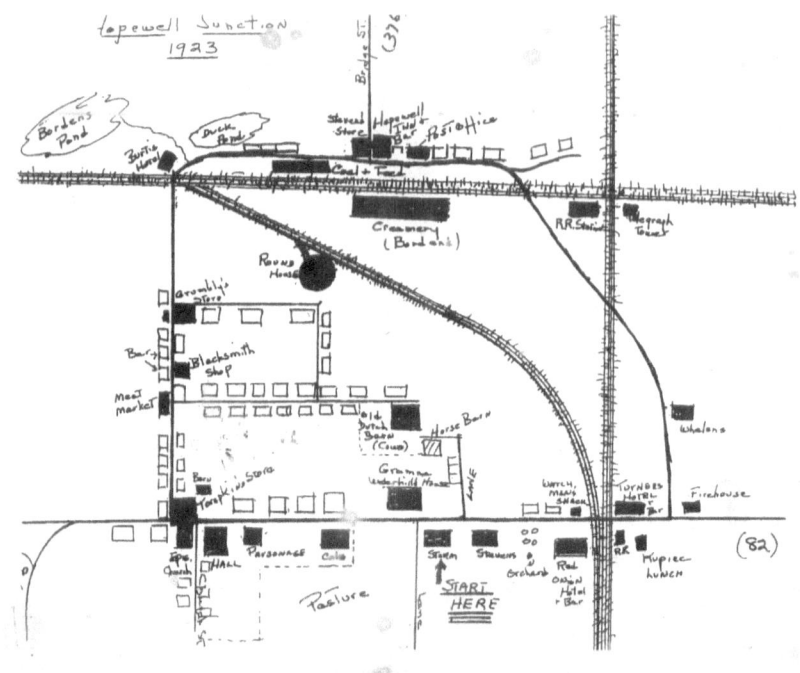

Charlotte Dodge's Saunter around Hopewell Junction 1923.

Today as usual, we wave to the engineer in the engine and again at the flagman in the caboose. We also had to wait for a little handcar which was pumped along the tracks by the workmen who prepared the switches.

Safely across the rails, we note a railroad freight building, and next to it is Cupette's lunchroom, which we rarely entered. The larger building across the street we gave wide berth to because we might meet up with someone who had been in the bar. It was a hotel run by Mr. Botsinturn, and assisted by his maiden daughter, Annie. Little did we realize that Annie would in World War II keep a jar urging donations on the counter for the soldiers. Not a boy from Hopewell who was in the service failed to receive gifts of cigarettes, candy, and sundries from her.

We now turn to the left, facing as we do the firehouse located in the corner. It has a large iron ring mounted outside, which is struck to announce a fire. To find the exact location of a fire, it was simple to ring

Central, who was the telephone operator. All of these buildings adjoining the railroad tracks were demolished when the overhead bridge was built, probably in 1935.

We cross more tracks, no watchman here, and come to the station where my Uncle Sam, Marie's father, was the station agent. This station is not bustling today since a passenger train has not long ago left for Poughkeepsie. We snoop around a bit, checking the roll of tickets, the lady's room, and avoiding the spittoons.

Our next stop is the post office, which is a building in a row of houses. It is a pretty active place because everyone in town picks up their mail there. As we enter, we are faced by a wall of boxes. Opening ours, we pick up any mail and proceed on our way.

We note that the Hopewell Inn is flourishing; it is an out-of-bounds place, too. Directly across is Borden's Creamery, where Ruth and Lee have a relative working, so we are welcome there. We encounter the unique odors of warm milk, ice, and sawdust. We are happy to receive a sliver of ice to munch on as we proceed on our way.

Woman and Children in Hopewell Junction Rail Yard. What is unique about this rail-yard image is that in the foreground and to the right a woman and a girl walk along a sidewalk between sets of tracks, and in the middle ground and center three boys sit on a pile of railroad ties. Usually, photos only show male workers on and around the tracks. Photograph from the Collection of J. W. Swanberg, Courtesy of J. W. Swanberg.

Living in Hopewell Junction | 93

We stop across the street at Steven's store to pick [up] a loaf of bread my mother has requested. Mr. Stevens is busy filling orders to be delivered, orders he has solicited by personal call on the telephone. The store is rather dark inside, with oiled wooden floor and dark walls and counters. No supermarket. There is a lot of merchandise in the store. On one side is the food market: canned goods, eggs, butter, bread. And on the other side: clothing, including shoes and overshoes, which were called "artics," and boots.

Across the road again we go on to the check out the feed and coal plant of my grandfather. He has died the year before, but I can still visualize him, seated at the roll-top desk working on accounts, a pipe in his mouth. The bins of feed and seed are fun to run your hands through.

Outside is the baked wooden scale flush with the ground, so wagons and trucks with their loads of coal can pull up and be weighed. It is one of life's marvels to me; since its weight registry is inside the office. I puff up with pride that my grandfather has such as wonderful invention.

Passing the shed and the duck pond, we come to Burtis' Hotel. There is a path between the building and pond, which leads to another pond, which is Borden's Creamery [pond] and is used for ice. "We never asked for permission to cut through Burtis' yard; it seemed to be a long-standing tradition [to cut through the yard]. The same is applied to Bate's yard on Orchard Street. On a sled, we slide under the fence and end up in Whitermen's yard.

Adults were kind and generous to us, and we were pretty well behaved, except, perhaps, on Halloween when a privy at the school was usually upset. Our good behavior was due in part to everyone knowing who we were and it being too easy to report any misbehavior back to our parents.

Crossing the tracks for the fourth time, we hear no whistle announcing the arrival of a train. The roundhouse is off to the left. We don't usually go in there: the big noisy engines are too intimidating, and, perhaps, the busy workmen do not have a welcome mat out for us, as this was the trains' hospital.

We do stop at Mr. Grumbly's store, however, where we have the change from the bread to spend. Mr. Grumbly is a bachelor of undisclosed age, somewhat of a recluse. He wears a wig held on by rubber bands. He has an ice-cream fountain in the store with typical ice-cream tables and chairs. He also sells magazines and newspapers, and in front of the store is a wonderful counter with candy. If I had a nickel to spend, it invariably goes for a roll of NECCO wafers. I especially liked the chocolate ones. It would be my turn when one of those appeared.

There was also a gasoline tank outside the store; Mary upset it one time, and someone else got on fire when a lighted match was thrown into a pool of spilled gas.

Mr. Grumbly saved his pennies, dumping them in a room upstairs. When he died, there were hundreds of pennies in this room. A barbershop was housed in a rear addition of the store and had its own entrance.

Mr. Grumbly also had a grocery store built next door. At the time of our walk, it housed the King's market, our first chain store. It was followed by the Schaffer store. In 1927, it would be run by Mr. and Mrs. Mc Keel. She is now Wilma Knickerbocker. Her children, Louis, Myra, and Ross, all three, are living in Hopewell. The tiny building across the way was perhaps a barbershop or maybe a shoe repair shop. We didn't stop, so I am not sure what was there.

Ahead was one of our favorite shops, the blacksmith run by Mr. Pascoe, George [Bailey's] grandfather. A fascinating place. The stamping of the horses, the switching of the tails, the hot fire pumped by the bellows until it is fiery red, the pounding of the anvil, and the hissing of the hot iron as it is dumped into water for cooling and hardening. And then the mystery of nailing the shoe onto the horse's hoof. He didn't even whimper or whine.

We didn't bother with the two bars across the street, and we didn't even bother stopping into Dan Lynch's meat market, although he was a very nice man.

It is getting late, and we were due home shortly. Sy Tomkins's store was on the corner. He has a well-known reputation of not being too generous. Wrapping all of his sales in a newspaper, he carried groceries as well as notions, buttons, and a bit of yarn goods. I am often asked by my grandmother to run down to the store for some item and am always glad to hear her say keep the change. Sy, too, had a counter of candies.

The Episcopal Church across the street, now Frankie's, is not our church, so we ignore it. Next is Aberdeen Hall. It is owned by the Dutch Reformed Church and is a familiar spot, this being our denomination.

There is a supper planned for this night in the basement, which houses the dining room and kitchen. Ladies are bustling around setting the tables.

The upstairs of the hall is used for various activities: Sunday-night church services, silent movies with Mr. Mill playing the piano, basketball games, plays, Christmas programs, and so forth. When an addition, a long room, stage, and kitchen, was put on the church, Aberdeen was sold to the Catholic church.

We pass the parsonage, and as we approached Mrs. Cole's house, her Wednesday club friends seem to be leaving. It is often my chore to guide them up the road or to stop the traffic. I leave the girls across from Mrs. Cole's and proceed on home. It is almost time for supper. I hope we will have fried potatoes; I sure do love them.

So, this is Hopewell Junction in 1923. And to me it is just like Lake Woebegone, where all the men are smart and all the women good-looking, and all the children are above average.

The End

The Lunds of Hopewell Junction: 1915–1963

Alfred Edward, Evert James, and David as Recollected by David Lund

My grandfather went to work for the Central New England Railroad in the Hopewell Junction railroad yard between 1915 and 1918. I am not sure exactly where he worked or what he did. Sometime between 1915 and 1918, he was involved in a railroad-car coupling accident in which he lost all or part of three fingers of his right hand. From then on in photographs, he always kept his right hand in his pocket or behind his body.

He stayed employed in the rail yard with the Central New England and later the New York, New Haven, and Hartford Railroad from 1918 to at least 1940 as a laborer in the engine house and eventually as a coal-pocket operator. In that last job, he shoveled coal, most likely at the coal pocket located in the southern end of the rail yard.

I think he shoveled coal at the coal pocket because of the watch he carried while working. I inherited the watch from him through my father,

Evert James Lund. I found it did not work all the time, so I took it to a watch repairer. He brought it back to me working well and all shined up. The watch repairer did mention to me that when he first opened up the watch, he found the inside full of black coal dust.

My grandfather lived just outside the east end of Hopewell Junction and used to walk to work. My father and his family including myself also lived outside of Hopewell Junction. My father was a carpenter who worked during the winter for the railroad at Hopewell Junction shoveling—not coal—snow off the tracks.

In the forties, my father became the fire chief of the Hopewell Junction Fire Department. He told me that the abandoned round house, in which engines were repaired, burned in 1949. My mother mentioned to me that while she was at [the] fire, she heard a pig scream in a house near the round house, so she went into the house, let the pig out, and watched it run down Railroad Avenue. The pig was never seen again, she said.

I remember in the mid-1950s a circus came to town. I also remember in the fifties and sixties that Hopewell Junction was not a dirty and loud town, probably because the railroad was mostly gone. It was a tiny town, and everybody knew everybody else. I am familiar with Charlotte Dodge's memoir of living in Hopewell Junction, and except for the railroad yard, I remember the hamlet much as she did.

By the early sixties, the IBM plant was built. At about the same time, the farms went out of business, and the farmers sold their fields to land developers. Hopewell Junction transformed from a railroader's town to a "Beamer" town and spread out from Railroad Avenue east and west along Route 82 and south down Route 376.

Vern Jackson: 1930s–1980s

I used to visit the station with my father. We delivered and picked up freight there. I first remember going with him when I was eight or ten, during the early 1940s.

My grandfather and father had an apple orchid, and we peddled the apples in Beacon. They stored the apples at La Grangeville. I sometimes rode with my father in the old truck from the farm to La Grangeville.

On the way back, I tried to get my father to race the steam train, but he never would.

We also took milk from the farm to Borden's [Creamery] for pasteurizing, separating the cream from the milk, and transporting it down to Beacon and [eventually] to New York City.

We put no cows in the stockyards for a train to pick them up. J. C. Penny loaded some of his cows in cars and transported them up to Rhinebeck to be shown at the Dutchess County Fair. After the fair, the cows were shipped back to the Penny farm.

If we had a delivery arrive at the station, the freight agent would either send a letter or call to let us know the delivery was there. For example, there might be a carload of feed to pick up. Once we bought a silo. It shipped from Marietta, Ohio. My father and I picked it up from the station. We had to have it trucked back to the farm.

We would drive to the station. The route was Jackson Road to the [Taconic State] Parkway, up the parkway to Route 82, down 82 to what is now 376, along 376 to Railroad Avenue, and by Railroad Avenue to the station. It was only about five miles from the farm to the station. It took fifteen to twenty minutes. It was not far away.

There we would enter one of the north-facing doors. Near the door, the agent would be in his office. The office was about eight feet by eight feet. There was a high counter in front of him, about three-and-a-half feet high, so a kid could not look over it at the agent.

The only agent whose name I remember was Mr. Cooper. I do not remember his first name. I have no idea if he was related to Liz Cooper, who was a station agent in the 1960s. He was not very big, but he was very accommodating. Mr. Cooper was there for many years.

On the west side of the station, there was a sliding door. We would back up a horse and wagon or the old truck to a ramp that ran down from the porch. We would carry, or roll, or slide the freight down and onto the wagon or truck.

I do not remember the round table at Hopewell Junction. I remember the repair shop burned up. The woods around here were cut down [for logs and lumber] and sold to the railroad. Diesels ruined everything for those of us who loved steam engines despite their steam and smoke. I hated to see them go.

I never rode the trains [from Hopewell Junction] to anywhere [Beacon, Danbury, or Poughkeepsie]. My wife's father caught the train at Fishkill Plains and rode it to Poughkeepsie High School. I saw a train wreck between the station and the rod-and-gun club. I stayed back fifty feet from it.

Because of the steam engines, the Hopewell Fire Company was putting out a lot of small fires every day. The fire company had a band. We could hear them play all the way out to the farm. We could hear train whistles and even the engines, too, at the farm. There was no other noise out at the farm.

The station was abandoned and soon closed. It was close to being torn down until that young fellow, Rich Taylor, built it back up again.

Mr. Jackson pointed to a framed map hanging on his dining-room wall. The map was dated 1868 and showed in dotted lines the path of a proposed railroad through the Town of East Fishkill. "There is the railroad that [eventually] ran beside the station," Mr. Jackson explained.

Barbara and James Moseman

Barbara Moseman

I was born in 1940 and was raised in Hopewell Junction. I lived on Orchid Place. I used to walk down the hill, pass the engine roundhouse on my left, and visit a person who lived on Bridge Street.

I remember the steam engines. When they would come into town, everyone would have to get their drying clothes off of the close lines to avoid being soiled again by the soot.

In the 1950s, my parents took me to Montgomery Wards department store in Poughkeepsie. They ordered a new bicycle for me. The clerk asked them where they lived, and when they said Hopewell Junction, the clerk said the bike would be delivered by train to the station there.

The bike arrived at the station sometime in August or September. I remember the station agent called us to say the bike was in and to pick it up. We walked in the south door of the station and picked up the bike. I remember the station agent was a man, but I do not remember where the bike was in the station. I rode that bike to the Old Hopewell Elementary School.

Hopewell Junction was a dirty, noisy town. To sit here in the depot today, the silence is strange. As I look out the windows of the depot today, I am always surprised to see a bike rider on the rail trail go by where the trains used to go by.

James Moseman

I lived in Glenham (a hamlet of Fishkill) in a rental house next door to the Texaco plant.

At the Glenham Railroad Station, near where I lived, the trains would come by loaded with pig iron. Only one-half of the train would go by at a time. The train would stop, the engine would be uncoupled from the freight cars, the engine would "turn around" on a siding, and it would head back to Beacon to pick up the other half of the train.

The reason for this complicated maneuver was the steep grade in the rail bed running just outside of Beacon and east up to Glenham. A train of fourteen cars carrying a heavy load, such as pig iron, could not make the grade all hitched together. So it would be broken into two parts.

Eventually, the engine would bring the other half of the train up to the first half. The engine would be uncoupled from the second half of the train, bypass the first half of the train on the siding, and be coupled up to the first car of the first half of the train. There would be fourteen cars altogether. Then the train would start out from Glenham east to Fishkill.

A fireman on one of the trains said he had to shovel extra coal into the boiler fire even to build up enough steam in the engine for it to drive up the grade just hauling a half train behind it. It was a tough pull, the fireman said, from Beacon to Glenham. Then the grade leveled off from Glenham on east to Hopewell Junction

I used to talk to the guys who hooked the two halves of the train together. I talked to the firemen, the brakemen, and the freight conductors. The engineers never talked to me. My father knew one of the engineers because of their common interest in baseball, so they would talk to each other. One of the engineers lived in Fishkill; his last name was Loop.

I told the guys with whom I spoke that I wanted to work for the railroad. They said forget about it, kid: the railroads are losing business and are disappearing.

Later, I worked at Texaco. One of my assignments was to test diesel engine oil. Alco Manufacturing built diesel engines. Alco complained that the engine oil they used caused the rings to stick and the bearings to wear down excessively. Texaco approached Alco to use their oil. Alco gave Texaco two diesel engines to test Texaco's oil. The diesels sat outside the plant.

I ran those engines 500 hours on Texaco oil. The rings did not stick, and the bearings did not wear down as much. Texaco reported these findings to Alco. Alco granted Texaco a contract to supply its oil to Alco. Alco passed on the Texaco report to all railroad lines advising those lines to contract with Texaco to supply them with the oil also.

When excursion trains occasionally ran from New Haven to Danbury, up to Hopewell Junction, and over to Beacon, my wife and I took them. We would board the trains in Danbury and ride through Hopewell Junction to Beacon. At Beacon, riders would get off the train, get on a bus, ride over to the foot of Mount Beacon, get off the bus, and get on the cog railroad that would pull them to the top of Mount Beacon for the view and the restaurant.

At the end of the day, the tourists, including ourselves, would ride the cog railroad, ride the bus, and ride the train back to Connecticut. Another trip went from Beacon south to Croton Harmon for a tour of the engine and car repair shops in the rail yard there.

Chapter 8

Working the Rails
1960–1974

The Phasing Out of Steam and the Phasing in of Diesels

Christian Wolmar calls the arrival of the diesel locomotive on the national railroad scene the "one last brave and flamboyant attempt to counter the threat of cars, [trucks,] and planes in an effort to try to retain the passenger [and freight] market" (309). Diesel locomotives were introduced into service as switcher engines in rail yards during the 1920s. Although, the diesels proved effective in the yards, they became even more successful on the long-haul main lines in the 1930s with passenger trains and in the 1940s with freight trains.

Diesels were more powerful and performed more efficiently than steam locomotives. They were built lighter and generated more power-to-weight ratio. They did not require coal pockets and water towers to replenish necessary fuel and water for steam and could be started and stopped immediately.

Diesel cabs were quieter, completely weatherproofed, cooler in summer, warmer in winter, and cleaner than the cabs of steam locomotives. One crew aboard a diesel locomotive could control multiple diesel units coupled behind the lead unit, while steam locomotives coupled together required multiple crews to operate each unit.

At Hopewell Junction, the NYNH&HRR planned in the late 1940s to replace the steam locomotives with diesel locomotives. The steam locomotives were employed as pusher engines to shoulder the long, heavy freight trains running east from Hopewell Junction to Danbury over Pauling Mountain. Two diesel locomotives positioned at the head of the train would haul the same freights without the need of a pusher engine positioned behind the caboose, except in the unusual instance of an extraordinarily long and heavily laden freight train.

A photograph taken in 1950 shows on the right Steam Locomotive #3558 and on the left a diesel locomotive. The steam locomotive was the last locomotive used as a pusher engine stationed at Hopewell Junction. It was retired in March 1951, after twenty-three years of service. Both locomotives are facing southeast to Danbury, Connecticut, and are located just beyond the County Route 82 overpass. To the left of the steam locomotive is the house in which sand was stored. Sand was spread on the rails in front of the locomotive, whether steam or diesel, to create traction

Two Types of Locomotives Working at Hopewell Junction. Photograph by Kent Cochrane in July 1950 from the Collection of J. W. Swanberg, Courtesy of J. W. Swanberg.

for the locomotive's trucks (railroad jargon for wheels), especially on steep slopes and in wet weather. The sand was applied to the tracks by a spreader located in front of the lead trucks of the locomotive. The sand house is still there, weathered and behind bushes.

The end of the steam locomotives at Hopewell Junction doomed all the buildings and structures that served them: the round table, the repair house, the water tower, and the coal pocket. The end of them also threatened the livelihood of the many employees who serviced the steam engines. According to an article in the *Poughkeepsie Journal*:

> It is estimated that 30 men will be affected but at least 10, and possibly more, will be able to take positions at other points on the line. [S]ome of the old-timers will hate to see the pushers go. The three pushers at the Hopewell yards have been there since 1918 and have been extensively used during that time, particularly during the two World Wars. Scheduled to be junked several years ago, they are still on the job. Now, it seems likely that they will find their way to the scrap pile.

Driving Trains through Hopewell Junction: Pete McLachlan

I have been interested in railroads since day one. I started in 1956 with the New Haven Railroad as an engine preparer. I helped service the engines in the Cedar Hill Yards in New Haven, Connecticut. My second day on the job, I was moving locomotives through the yard. Soon after, I was transferred to Danbury, Connecticut, as a turn-table operator. I helped rotate the table with two other men by hand.

Then I was driving pusher engines out of Danbury and up the Maybrook Line which ran through Hopewell Junction, to help the freight trains get over the mountain [Pauling Mountain] at Whaley Lake. Once the freights were over the mountain and headed toward Hopewell Junction, I would back down the pusher engine to the Danbury Yard.

In 1959, I was promoted to fireman, and, in 1965, I was promoted to engineer. The New Haven Railroad was a good railroad. No radios on the trains, no kerosene lamps on the switches, and sixteen-hour work days until 1972 when the work day went down to fourteen hours a day. No social life. But it was a good railroad.

When we came through Hopewell Junction, we ran fast. Either we were slowing down from coming down the mountain at Whaley Lake, or we were gathering up speed to get up over the mountain. By fast I mean up to fifty miles per hour. We would run up to 150 freight cars of all types through Hopewell Junction. Occasionally, we would drop something off, for example lumber to the yard just south of the station.

As we came through Poughkeepsie and approached the Highland-Poughkeepsie Bridge, we slowed to twelve miles per hour to go over the bridge. We could cross the bridge in not less than seven minutes. There were three clocks on the bridge to time us, and all three were accurate.

At the bridge, I would release the air brakes on each car so as to bunch up the cars. Then I would let the engine pull the cars over the bridge. After the engine was off the bridge, I began to speed up again for there was a grade going through Highland. When the caboose was off the bridge, I would set the air brakes again.

Once, when I was still a fireman on trains going over the bridge, the engineer stopped the train in the middle of the bridge. He was not supposed to do that. Oil would drip down from the cars and off the bridge. If the train was over land, and there were houses under the bridge, the oil would land on the roofs and sides of the buildings. Then, the railroad would have to pay to clean them

Anyway, the engineer told me to get off the train and use the telephone on the bridge. I got off the engine ok, but when I looked down, I was scared. So, to get to the telephone, I slid along on my rear end. I am scared of heights. That is why I will not go up on the Walkway over the Hudson today.

Back to Hopewell Junction, when I drove work trains through there, I would have to wait for the freights to go by whether they were traveling west to Maybrook or east to Danbury.

Occasionally, we would climb down from the train and visit with Liz Cooper, the station agent. She was very lady-like. When she walked into a room, we would all get up. We would never use vulgar language in her presence.

However, one day, the freight conductor said within her hearing something about he was not going to wait any longer to pick up some f——-g cattle waiting in the stockyard at Hopewell. Liz turned to him and said, "When you are finished f——-g with the cattle, load them into the cars."

The last time I stopped in Hopewell Junction while still on salary, the train master, not Liz Cooper, had a box of sandwiches from S. S. Pierce. There had been an event the night before in Hopewell, and the sandwiches were left over. They were still good. He offered them to us. Great sandwich.

In my career, I ran all sorts of engines: steam, diesel, and electric. I retired on October 28, 1998. When I was aboard trains, I took along a camera to take pictures of railroads. Today, I lecture and present slide shows. I am also a docent at the Railway Museum in Danbury.

By the way, when we would run through Hopewell Junction in the 1980s, we would look at the station and say, "Give it its last rites and tear it down." But Bernie Rudberg and all the volunteers who worked to restore the depot, build the signal tower, and develop the museum have done a wonderful job. I am glad no one gave the depot its last rites.

Firing Trains through Hopewell Junction 1960s: Jack Swanberg

I have heard the expression that you do not choose a passion; it chooses you. My passion is railroads. I have always been a railroad buff. My father commuted from Darien, Connecticut, to Manhattan. My sister and I watched him come and go on the train.

I graduated from Trinity College in Hartford, Connecticut, in June 1961 and managed to get a job as a fireman on the New Haven Railroad in August 1961. My parents were disappointed with me. Here I was a college graduate, yet I wanted to work on the railroad. I knew I would be drafted in a year. So, I wanted to spend that year working on the railroad. Eventually, in the fall of 1962, I entered the navy for four years. In 1966, I was released from active duty in naval aviation.

A fireman on a diesel locomotive checks the units [engines] for overheating. He also checks the sanders that provide sand for traction of the wheels on steep grades, checks fuel levels, fills the big water jug for drinking water, and cuts ice for the water jug. On steam locomotives, the fireman tends the fire for the boiler by feeding it wood or coal. That is where the term comes from.

In 1961, the New Haven Railroad had 0400 series diesels. They had been bought in 1947. The sanders were unreliable, the units could overheat, and the high-pressure fuel lines leaked. These would have to be repaired by hand on the spot.

There were no two-way radios, so communication among the crew was by hand signals only. The crew on the train usually included five men: the engineer, fireman, and head brakeman up front in the cab and the rear brakeman and freight conductor back in the caboose.

In New York State, a sixth man, a second head brakeman, was required. The train would slow way down in Danbury, and this brakeman would swing onto the train for the ride to Maybrook, New York. Thus, he was known as the swing man.

In 1961, the Maybrook line had only a single track and sidings. At Hopewell Junction, New York, the west-bound trains would sometimes have to wait for the east-bound to pass through.

As the train came up to Hopewell, there would be an approach signal indicating a stop signal ahead. The engineer would slow to thirty mph and be prepared to stop at the next signal. If the train had one hundred or more cars, the engineer could not come to a sudden stop. We would stop just before the Route 82 overpass. That was the place west-bound trains halted. By the way, west-bound trains were odd-numbered trains; east-bound were even numbered.

At Hopewell Junction, there used to be kerosene lamps by the switches, so they could be easily seen. However, there was no one there to maintain the lamps. They were replaced by reflectors. That worked okay in the headlights of the head unit. It did not work okay if the engineer was backing up the train to drop off or pick up cars by the lumber yard.

At Hopewell, there was the station, the depot that has been restored. A station agent would come out of the station and wave us on as we went by at full speed, which, at Hopewell Junction was 40 mph, according to the employees' timetable. The guy would also signal to the rear brakeman on the caboose if there was anything wrong with the cars, such as a hot box that the brakeman could not see. A hot box is an overheated axel on the rolling stock of a train.

We never stopped in Hopewell Junction to buy food. We packed enough food for a sixteen-hour trip from New Haven's Cedar Hill Yards to Maybrook. Today there are just twelve-hour days. However, at Holmes, New York, a hamlet within the town of Pawling, just over the Putnam County line, there was a grocery store right where the tracks crossed the road. If we had to stop there, we got some food, but, otherwise, we just roared right through. We never stopped just for refreshments, but, if we had to stop to meet an opposing freight, we would find a local food store if one was available.

As a fireman, I ran the train part of the time. At the New Haven Railroad, you needed ten years of seniority to become an engineer. Training was on the job, so the way you became a fireman or an engineer was by doing it.

Driving a train over a flat grade is easy. Driving over a down grade is hard. You must watch for slack action between the cars. You must control the air brakes through the downgrades.

After my release from active duty in naval aviation in 1966, I became a management trainee at the New York Central Railroad from 1966 to 1968. From 1968 to 1976, I was assistant trainmaster then trainmaster at Penn Central Railroad. From 1976 to 1983, I was trainmaster for Consolidated Rail Corp. From 1983 to 2000, I was trainmaster then lead trainmaster for Metro-North Railroad.

I retired on January 1, 2000, after thirty-eight years working on the railroad. Not always easy, but a rewarding career indeed. I still write articles about and take pictures of railroads and publish them in *Railroad History* and *The Shoreliner*. The research for my book *New Haven Power, 1838–1968: Steam, Diesel, Electric, MU's, Trolleys, Motor Cars, Buses and Boats* is at the University of Connecticut.

Hopewell Junction Depot Station Agents: Elizabeth Cooper and Thomas DeJoseph

The first time I can recall being around trains is when I was three-and-a-half years old in 1953. My father worked for Pepperidge Farms. In 1953, he was sent to Cincinnati, Ohio, to determine if stores in the Midwest would stock Pepperidge Farm breads on their shelves. My father would go to the Cincinnati Railroad Station and wait for the cars to come in carrying the bread.

He took me and my two older brothers with him to the station. I can still see the Norfolk and Western train with its stream-lined steam engine pulling into the station as if it had pulled in today. I recall saying with astonishment that the wheels on the locomotive "are bigger than I am." I like the idea of these monstrous machines providing economic value to the county.

In 1967, I was hired to sell train tickets for the New Haven Railroad at the station in Westport, Connecticut. I worked only four days when I received a call from my supervisor. She told me to go home. She just found out I was only seventeen. Connecticut State law, she said, asserts that only those eighteen years and older can work around heavy machinery. While I was only selling tickets now, I might be asked to go outside the station and be around the trains, and that would be breaking the law. I suppose she was only CYA.

Not even a year later, on January 8, 1968, when I turned eighteen, I again applied for a job at the NHRR, I again was accepted, and I was posted at the Danbury station on the day shift. By "posted," I mean I was learning on the job and was studying the *Book of Rules* to take the exam to become an inter-locking operator. The *Book of Rules* contains all the regulations of the road for operating trains. I passed the exam in February 1968. An "interlocking operator" understands the combination of railroad switches and signals, manages these combinations, and carries them out.

For example, in the station, the operator sets the signal aspect at the end of a block to the color red. A "block" is a section of track between two stations. Next, the operator pulls the lever to engage both switches. The first switch allows a train to leave one track, and the second switch allows that train to enter another track perhaps two or three over from the first track. Third, the operator releases the red signal aspect as the train goes on its way. No movement by a train from one track to another is allowed unless the signal aspect at the back of the block is set to red.

My first meeting or, rather, encounter, with Pete McLachlan was when I was new to the job. Pete walks in and tells me he will take both sets of train orders. "Train orders" are the work assignments for a particular train. Usually, two sets of orders are made up by the station agent, one for the engineer and one for the conductor. I refused to give him both sets of orders because I needed to hand the second set to the conductor, who was not there at the same time as Pete.

Pete said, "Look, sonny. Just give me both orders. The conductor might be riding up in the cab with me, and I will give him his set." I still refused because the *Book of Rules* stated that only one set went to the engineer. And one set is all I gave Pete. I succeeded but incorrectly. Pete and I are great friends today, although we got off to a rocky start. I was re assigned to several stations, usually as a fill in for those agents who had not had a vacation in a long time, up to four years in some cases. So, in June 1968, I was assigned to the depot at Hopewell Junction. I relieved Mrs. Elizabeth Cooper. She was delighted to have someone relieve her. She showed me her duties and responsibilities. For example, she took me on her various railroad errands cashing checks made out to the railroad by various local customers and visiting some of those customers to determine their orders and the cars by which to deliver their orders.

At the depot, the room where the museum is located now was filled with stuff. Some of it may have been things used by the signal-maintenance workers, some of it may have been freight, and some of it may just have been junk. The offices and the room where volunteers greet visitors were well kept by Liz. I assume those rooms were neat because a trainmaster might suddenly show up for an unannounced inspection of the station and because of a woman's touch.

I do not remember that the safe now in the freight office was the one with which I worked; that safe was much taller than the one in the depot now. I never used the telegraph because I never learned Morse Code, and messages never came over that machine. Of course, I used the telephone to talk with customers, freight-car distributers, and freight-car locators. I do not remember the stove now in the visitors' room.

I worked at the depot in Hopewell Junction only three weeks total in June 1968. I remember coal cars, oil cars, and some sort of winery tank car going to the Clinton Winery. Coal cars were dropped off at a siding for the Green Haven Prison. Twelve trains came through Hopewell Junction, six going east and six going west, along with one train, a local, coming up from Beacon and delivering bricks to Montfort and material to the IBM plant. That local also picked up "hot" cars loaded with freight to be delivered and "cold" cars empty of freight to be sent back.

When Liz returned from vacation, I went to New Milford, Connecticut. I never was re-assigned to Hopewell Junction. Instead, I worked at the station in Danbury; I worked as the tower operator up in the signal tower in Stanford. As far as I know, Liz Cooper may be the last station agent assigned to the Depot at Hopewell Junction.

Working on the Rails: Howard Beneway, Jr.

I was hired by the New York, New Haven, and Hartford railroad in 1959 and retired in 1984 when the tracks running from Poughkeepsie to Hopewell Junction were pulled up and the depot was abandoned.

I helped repair rails. On the curves, the high, or outside, rail would wear thin. We would replace that rail with the low, or inside, rail that was thicker. We would do that just once. If either the high or low rail needed replacement again, we would replace it with a new rail. On straightaways, we would notice a dip in a rail. Then we would jack that rail up and build up underneath the rail with more rail bed.

On bridges, especially the Poughkeepsie-Highland Bridge over the Hudson River, we would replace the ties, timbers eighteen inches by sixteen inches. Some of those ties were still there after that bridge burned. If we were working on a bridge, and we heard the engine whistle blow, we would get off the tracks and onto the catwalk. I don't think the engineers liked us that much: they would just stare down at us without smiling or even waving.

To let an engineer know we were working on the tracks, we would fasten four "torpedoes" to the track both ahead and behind where we were working. Two torpedoes were attached on each rail in staggered formation. When the engine trucks [wheels] rolled over a torpedo it would explode. The loud sound would tell the engineer to slow down or even stop before the track work.

One time, while we were pulling up a rail an early train approached. Either we had not set the torpedoes, or the engineer did not hear them.

We heard the whistle. So, we quickly hammered the spikes back into the rail to push the partially raised rail back onto the ties. We managed to hammer in all the spikes. But there was no place to get away from the tracks in case the rail did not hold and the cars derailed. We just stood beside the tracks and watched that rail go up and down, and the spikes gradually rise up. We thought we were goners. We were so happy finally to see that caboose go by.

I remember some wrecks. We would spend all night lifting cars and repairing track. We used steam cranes to hoist the derailed cars because steam cranes were stronger than diesel cranes. It took three men to lift and place a raising hook under a derailed car before the car could be lifted up and onto the tracks.

One wreck was caused by a young engineer who backed up a train, released the air brakes, started the train forward without putting the air brakes on again, and the cars ran into one another. Another wreck happened at Whaley Lake when a train jumped a rail on a siding. There were no fuel leaks if an engine derailed.

We kept a lot of tools and other materials at the Hopewell Junction depot. The west side of the depot had a big sliding barn door. What used to be the west waiting room was filled with barrels of spikes and bolts, tools, and big barrels of grease—until we stopped using grease.

Henry Cooper was the station agent. He sat at a desk in what was the east waiting room near the windows facing south. He was the quiet type. In the afternoon, he would phone to the station agent in Danbury, Connecticut, to see if there were any trains coming up or down the tracks between Danbury and Poughkeepsie. If there were none, and if my section gang was around the depot, he would send us home after 3:30.

Besides track repair, we did other jobs. I worked track patrol with another man; we worked in pairs. We would do different small repairs that did not need a section gang. Once I rescued a baby deer—a Bambi—took it home with me, and raised it as a household pet. We would spray fifty-five-gallon cans of calcium at every railroad crossing to keep down bushes and trees. We sprayed 500 hundred feet on either side of the crossing.

In 1965, I got sick. I could not slow my heart down. I stayed in the house and went from 184 pounds to 152 pounds. A doctor injected me with just one type of medicine; I had no other medicine given to me.

The railroad wanted to keep my condition quiet. They compensated me while I was on sick leave. I was coaxed by my co-workers to get out of the house, walk the tracks, and ride in the maintenance car. By 1966, I was back to work.

Sometimes I worked switch duty at night. Then I slept all alone in the Hopewell Junction depot, or if I was assigned to east of the Maybrook [Orange County] Railroad Yard, I slept all alone in a shed with a wood stove. I wore earphones to hear the dispatcher at Maybrook tell me if a train was coming and if I needed to switch it to another track or siding. Once a train came early, but I did not have to switch it off to another track. It was snowing, so when the train passed the shack, the rocking cars looked like monsters swaying by me.

If I was working near Fishkill Plains and my car was parked at the Hopewell Junction depot, I would walk to the siding where the pusher engines were. If a pusher engine was leaving the siding to head south and help a train up and over Pauling Mountain, I would hitch a ride with the engineer and jump off at the depot to pick up my car and drive home.

One afternoon, I was working on the switch to the spur into the Green Haven Prison. I parked my Metro-North truck just before the switch. I was out of the cab repairing the switch, paying attention to that more than anything else, when I felt a dog's teeth and strong jaw clamp down on my wrist. I stopped still. Then I heard a voice behind me say, "If you don't move, I will tell the dog to release you." I did not move, and the dog let go of my wrist.

The voice said, "You can stand up." I did. "Turn around," it said. I did that, too. The voice belonged to a prison guard from Green Haven. He had his gun out and pointed at me.

"What are you doing here?" he asked me.

"I was sent to repair this switch, so freight trains can go down the spur and into the prison."

The guard said, "You're right. I opened your cab door and saw your work order on the driver's seat."

I didn't say anything, but I was relieved and happy he said that.

"Look," the guard said. "The next time the railroad must do work on the spur inside or outside the prison, let us know. We won't hassle you; we'll help you if we can."

The guard left with his dog. "You have a good day," he said.

When he had disappeared behind a gate, I felt behind my back where I kept a gun tucked into my belt. It was registered. I pack it in case I run into a coyote—or a wolf. I have dropped one of those when I have been working.

So I went back to work, fixed the switch, and left with a story to tell you.

Chapter 9

More Rails Depart Hopewell Junction

Another Assortment of Boardroom Mergers

As with many railroads large and small, in over four decades, from 1927 to 1969, the NYNH&HRR weakened, rallied, deteriorated, and then failed. In 1961, it went bankrupt. As a result of a lack of business, it pulled up one of its double tracks on the Maybrook line running from the Poughkeepsie-Highland Bridge; through Hopewell Junction; to Danbury, Connecticut.

In 1968, two of the largest railroads in financial poor health, the PRR and the NYCRR merged to make the Penn Central Railroad (PCRR). By themselves, the two former railroads believed their merger would save their combined assets. However, the Interstate Commerce Commission compelled the PCRR to take in the bankrupt and failing NYNH&HRR, including its once-prized Poughkeepsie-Highland Bridge on January 1, 1969. The PCRR was not interested in the bridge because it did not like the antiquated Maybrook Rail Yard where east-bound trains were formed. The PCRR preferred the state-of-the-art Selkirk Rail Yard and the relatively new Selkirk-Castleton Bridge where east-bound trains were also formed over the Hudson River just south of Albany. Selkirk

was more efficient than the Maybrook yard. It classified cars electronically, breaking the cars as they came down the yard's hump, not by hand but by automatic retarding. It had up-to-date facilities for rail-truck container interchange. Routing through the Selkirk yard was also better because long-distance traffic coming east through Selkirk would likely arrive on Penn Central tracks. Traffic coming east through Maybrook would reach there by other independent railroads, such as the Erie-Lackawanna [. . .] and only from there move by Penn Central tracks, for a shorter haul. (Mabee 242)

Two years after the PCRR was formed, in 1971, it went bankrupt itself due to an incompetent, unproductive management of its railroad system and lack of government financial support (Mabee 243).

The reorganization of the PCRR consisted of maintaining the Maybrook Rail Yard and re-assigning personnel to various locations including four track workers to Hopewell Junction. It provided for the first time two-way radios on the trains for the crew to talk to each other and to stations along the way. It repaired the Beacon-to-Hopewell Junction Branch to manage the increase in traffic coming from the Selkirk Rail Yard, over the Selkirk-Castleton Bridge, down the east side of the Hudson River, through Poughkeepsie to Beacon, then up to Hopewell Junction, and across to Danbury (Mabee 244).

The Dutchess County businesses served by the PCRR in the 1970s are not necessarily familiar names in 2021. The freight delivered varied, and Carleton Mabee itemizes some items: "Western Publishing—paper, Smith Brothers Cough Drops—syrup, Effron Bakery—flour, Dutton—lumber, Hudson River Psychiatric Hospital—coal, Poughkeepsie city—salt, [. . .] Miron—lumber, Green Haven prison—coal, flour, feed [. . .]" (243). Some of these places, such as the Hudson River Hospital, Smith Brothers Cough Drops, and Western Publishing, have vanished like the railroad that served them and the spur tracks over which it ran.

In 1976, Conrail, a corporation conceived by the US Congress took over a number of failing railroads in the northeast, including the PCRR. Conrail was charged by Congress to carry on without federal help and to stop and abandon all unprofitable railroads. It did both. For example, it pulled up the track running from Poughkeepsie to Hopewell Junction in 1984.

Dutchess County, in turn, bought the trackless right of way from Conrail, buried water lines underground, and paved the rail bed to create a rail trail following the course of the original tracks. The HRR bought the Beacon Branch running from Beacon through Hopewell Junction to Danbury, Connecticut. It planned to run freight trains serving nearby customers located along the line. Metro-North bought the Beacon Branch. It planned to "bank" the branch as an alternative track shuttling commuter trains from the Hudson River line to the Harlem River Line if a blockage occurred on either line between Dutchess County and either Putnam or Westchester counties, according to Jack Swanburg, who by now was train master for Metro-North. The Danbury Railroad Museum occasionally ran round-trip excursion trains from Danbury to Beacon as late as the early 2000s for passengers to climb Mount Beacon or enjoy the fall foliage. Otherwise, the tracks were silent.

The Poughkeepsie-Highland Railroad Bridge Burns

At about two o'clock May 8, 1974, black smoke lifted from the east, or Poughkeepsie, side of the Poughkeepsie-Highland Railroad Bridge, billowed into a gray cloud, and spread along the length of the bridge. The wood smoke came from the burning railroad ties and the burning wooden walkway running alongside the ties. The eighty-six-year-old bridge was ending its useful railroad career in a spectacular but inglorious blaze.

No maintenance workers were stationed on the bridge. No fire was immediately reported to firehouses on both sides of the river. People on the ground noticed the smoke and turned in alarms. Fireman soon discovered that despite their engines positioned on land and directly under the bridge, their pumps, hoses, and water streams failed to reach even the lower side of the bridge. Going up on top of the bridge itself, the firemen almost immediately discovered that despite turning on the valves of the bridge's waterline, they failed to produce water. Carleton Mabee explains this failure as the result of the steel pipeline, "Not [having] been drained the previous winter it had burst in several points—PCRR had known it but not repaired it" (247).

Suspended above the river in a cloud of thick smoke, the fireman found it difficult to know what was burning and where to step in order not to burn themselves or fall through the bridge to the river below. The fire's heat bent rails, twisted girders, and shimmied the bridge itself. Shaken loose by the fire, pieces of the bridge dropped down on land and water. Spikes, plates, and rivets banged on the roofs of houses, thudded into lawns, and splashed into the river, setting all solid surfaces on fire and steaming the water. Metal debris clogged the Hudson River Railroad line and blocked local streets. Nearly five hours later, the fireman declared the bridge fire to be out (Mabee 247).

Like the smoke billowing around the bridge, speculation as to who or what bore responsibility for the fire soon started and ballooned about the event. Was the cause the failure of PCRR to repair the water main, to position maintenance people on the bridge, and to assign guards to look out for the railroad's property? Were these failures an issue of negligence or deliberate intention on the part of the railroad? No authorized, bureaucratic examination into the causes of the fire occurred.

Mabee explores conceivable effects to the bridge fire:

> Certainly [. . .] some Penn Central's officials, as they understood its interests, welcomed the fire. Penn Central, weak as it was, had not wanted to take over the ailing New Haven Railroad along with its Poughkeepsie Bridge, but federal officials had forced it to. It was costly for Penn Central to operate both the Poughkeepsie and Selkirk [b]ridges and their accompanying rail yards. [. . .] Penn Central, if it took a narrow view of its interests, would find it to its advantage to concentrate on using the modern Selkirk yard and its related Selkirk-Castleton Bridge and welcome an excuse to abandon the outmoded Maybrook yard and its related Poughkeepsie Bridge. (248–49)

Whether Mabee's point of view was PCRR's thinking or not, the bridge, or what was left of it, was abandoned, and the Selkirk rail yard and bridge were kept and used.

One other casualty that took place that May afternoon was a dream of owning a house. Howard Beneway remembers that "[o]n that afternoon, I got a call from my boss telling me that the Bridge had burned, that I close the depot, and that I work out of Danbury from now on. I had just put down a deposit on a house on Railroad Avenue. I told the bank, and, fortunately, they gave me back my deposit. I was free to keep my old house."

Pulling Up the Rails from Poughkeepsie to Hopewell Junction: Dave Williams, an Eyewitness

The last revenue run of Conrail on the Poughkeepsie-to-Hopewell Junction track never made Hopewell. The *Poughkeepsie Switcher* ran on April 5, 1982, and stopped only at Miron Lumber, Quinlan Gas, and Page Home and Hardware Center. Miron is located on the Titusville Road, while Quinlan is located on the Old Manchester Road, and Page on Manchester Road.

The last ever run of Conrail on the Poughkeepsie-to-Hopewell Junction track definitely made Hopewell. The work train pulled up the rails from Poughkeepsie to Hopewell Junction. I did not watch the crew pull up the track every day, but I took notes on the crew's daily progress. The train's crew was twenty-five men. I did have two black flags that some trains display on the engine of a final run to suggest something like mourning for the railroad. I asked the guys if they would display the flags. They said, "Okay. Climb up on the engine and fasten the flags."

The work train left the Selkirk Yard on March 5, 1984. [Selkirk is a large railroad yard for freight situated in Selkirk, New York, eight miles south of Albany. Now owned by CSX Transportation, the yard is the main freight yard for the northeast, including destinations along the Hudson River down to New York City.] The train included an engine, a box car carrying tools, several flat cars to pick up the pulled-up rails, and a caboose.

The train ran down to Poughkeepsie, next further down to Beacon, then up to Hopewell Junction on the Beacon Branch. When it arrived in Hopewell, it went just east of the Route 82 overpass. After that it backed up all the way to the Creek Road underpass in Poughkeepsie.

Before the train had arrived to pull up the tracks, a four-man crew started walking from Creek Road south to Hopewell Junction marking the sections of track. Behind that crew was another four-man crew pulling up spikes from every fifth or sixth tie and leaving just two spikes in the ties to let the train pass over the rails at walking speed.

Once at Creek Road, on the very same day it arrived there, the train began to move forward again, and the crew began to pull up the track from Creek Road to North Grand Avenue. That day it snowed. But the next day, March 6, the snow melted, and it did not snow again until March 14. The next day, the crew pulled up the track from North Grand Avenue to the Arlington Siding by the Route 44 overpass. March 7, the crew pulled up the track from the Arlington Siding to the Noxon Road overpass. March 8, they pulled up track from Noxon Road to Mile Post 37 near Miron Lumber.

While the train was parked near Miron, a garbage truck crashed into one of the rail cars. Nobody knew it at first except me and a train buddy of mine who saw it happen because the engine crew was up in the engine, and the track crew was standing farther back of the train.

It took another seven days, until March 15, for the train to reach Hopewell Junction and the last of the track to be pulled up. It snowed the day before, and it was still on the ground because of the bitter cold. The engine pulled the rail cars to the 82 bridge where the rail cars were in front of the depot.

The depot by then was boarded up since before 1984. The crew did not pay attention to it. The only sound at the front of the train was the engine idling, while at the back of the train it was very noisy and dirty.

Before the tracks were pulled up, state road crews took down all the grade-crossing lights and signs. So, Conrail had to put up signs again signifying that the track was a live track and drivers should be cautious when approaching the grade crossing.

Another Fire and the Abandonment and Near Destruction of the Hopewell Junction Depot

Between the burning of the Poughkeepsie-Highland Railroad Bridge in 1974 and the pulling up of the railroad tracks from Poughkeepsie to Hopewell Junction in 1984, the depot was neglected. Track workers

The Hopewell Junction Depot Shortly after the Fire. A photograph by Austen McEntee of the Hopewell Junction Depot in 1986 shortly after the fire and before Metro-North boarded up the depot for the second time. The depot remained in this squalid condition until Rich Taylor discovered the almost unrecognizable building in 1994. Photograph from the Collection of J. W. Swanberg, Courtesy of J. W. Swanberg.

occasionally used the building to store tools and track-repair materials; otherwise, it remained deserted and ignored. Eventually, just before the tracks were pulled up, Metro-North boarded up the windows, locked the doors permanently, and let the exterior and interior deteriorate.

In 1986, two years after Metro-North left the depot to the weather and the weeds, it was set on fire. Who started the fire, how, and why remain shrouded in smoke, so to speak. Residents noticed the flames and smoke and called the fire department. To put out the fire and perhaps to save the approximately 106-year-old building, firefighters broke down doors, cut holes into the roof, and smashed windows. Most of the fire damage occurred in the west end of the depot, although the entire interior suffered considerable smoke damage. The ruined, aging depot survived.

After the fire, Metro-North once again nailed plywood over the door frames and windows. There were no doors to lock permanently. The roof was not covered even by a tarpaulin, so the interior deteriorated more rapidly than before due to weather exposure.

Chapter 10

Restoring the Depot

How, then restore an abandoned, bordered-up, fire-scarred railroad depot? To paraphrase Christian Wolmar in *The Great Railroad Revolution*, whose opinion on what is required to build a railroad is cited in the beginning of chapter 1:

> There are several elements that [must] come together: the technology to demolish, repair, and refurbish; the financing to pay for the technology and the new materials; the creation of the appropriate legal framework; and, of course, the labor, voluntary if possible, for restoration. Such coordination of different agencies, technologies, and resources require[s] vision and ambition, as well as the cooperation of the various entities involved. It is hardly surprising, therefore, that the emergence of the restoration of the Hopewell Junction Depot, the founding of the Hopewell Junction Depot Museum, and the recognition of the Hopewell Junction Depot as a National Historic Site was a stuttering process, conducted in fits and starts with numerous failures and dead ends. (2)

The following accounts of the restoration of the Hopewell Junction Depot are essentially an accompaniment of oral histories by several of the volunteers who restored the depot. Their accounts report their failures and dead ends as well as their successes and completions.

First Glance: Richard Taylor

I first became interested in the depot in September 1994 when I came over to Philip Ortiz's on Railroad Avenue in Hopewell Junction to have some welding done on my truck. From across Ortiz's cluttered yard, I saw this dilapidated building that looked like it might have been a train station. I asked a worker if he knew what the building was. He said he guessed it was a railroad station. I instantly knew this building had to be saved and restored. The next day I came back and took pictures of what I was to learn was the Hopewell Junction depot.

The area around the depot was used as storage with piles of large pipes and steel panels. The place where the depot was located was unattractive with other rundown buildings surrounding it, a short road run-

The Dilapidated Hopewell Junction Depot in 1994. Photograph by Richard Taylor from the Collection of Richard and Maureen Taylor, Courtesy of Richard and Maureen Taylor.

ning past it and dead ending at an abandoned railroad bed, and a junk yard sprawling on the other side of the railroad bed. No wonder no one seemed interested in it.

I spent 1995 trying to get railroad buffs interested in restoring the depot and setting it up as a railroad museum. No one seemed interested. I came up with another idea of contacting people out of the area. I contacted Jack Swanburg, who had been a fireman on trains running through Hopewell Junction and who lives in Connecticut. Jack encouraged me to write articles in the local newspapers and said he would place an article in one of the publications of the New Haven Railroad Historical and Technical Association, Inc.

In February 1996, I placed a notice in both the *Poughkeepsie Journal* and the *Southern Dutchess News* announcing two meetings to be held at the East Fishkill Library, not far from and within walking distance of the depot. The notice stated that I was not only interested in preserving the structure of the depot but also interested in preserving the history of Hopewell Junction.

Jack Swanberg's advice on publicity paid off. Twenty-six people showed up to my first meeting. That evening two people signed up to be on the steering committee. At the second meeting, two more people volunteered to work on the steering committee. Business owners, carpenters, historians, painters, railroad buffs, and just interested citizens filled the meeting room at the East Fishkill Library.

First Effort: Bernard T. Rudberg

In the winter of 1996, a group of local citizens decided to do something about the deteriorating condition of the Hopewell Junction depot. They met at the East Fishkill Library after seeing a notice in either the *Poughkeepsie Journal* or the *Southern Dutchess News* written by Rich Taylor. The group formed a non-profit organization called the Hopewell Depot Restoration Corporation (HDRC). The objective, as Rich's notice stated, was to save the depot and to turn it into a small museum and educational facility.

The HDRC began trying to raise funds to meet its twin goals. Nearly eighteen months later, in August 1997, The Dutchess County Legislature agreed to sell the depot building to the HDRC for the lofty sum of one dollar! The Legislature also agreed to a fifteen-year renewable lease on the land under the building.

Once the HDRC took possession of the depot, we wanted to look inside. So we began by pulling the plywood off the window frames both to let light into the building for the first time since 1986 and to peek through the windows to see what objects if any were still in the depot. What we saw was black as charcoal with rain- and snow-soaked debris drenched from the gaping holes in the roof.

The group was discouraged by the dismal sight. Nevertheless, we began work by nailing sheets of recycled plywood over the roof holes and placing a tarpaulin over the whole roof. Over the next thirteen years of the restoration, we replaced tarps every year because they lasted only one year.

There was very little salvageable material inside the depot. Among the items tossed out was the rusting hulk of a 1960s-era oil burner. For some strange reason, the railroad had poured about two inches of concrete over the old floor. Of course, it was cracked. Volunteers swung sledgehammers and strained backs to break up the concrete. They loaded the broken pieces into wheelbarrows and hauled the heavy loads out the doors of the building.

Almost all the walls had to be cleaned of the charcoal, a residue of the fire. Wooden racks used by the railroad signal crew crumbled to the touch and were removed. The basement was wet and partially filled with sand washed in by the rain from the old railroad bed next to the depot. We shoveled the sand into the same wheelbarrows as we loaded the broken concrete and hauled out those heavy loads. In the basement, was another rusting hulk, a coal-burning furnace this time. We pulled it up the basement stairs and pushed it out the door and sold it for scrap metal.

The sills of the building were rotted after years of resting in dirt and mud. We bolted large, laminated beams to the walls and used house jacks to raise the building up high enough to repair and replace the rotting sills. Inside, we held up the old floor with a salvaged section of discarded rail from the tracks that once ran past the depot. During most of 2003 and 2004, we rebuilt the floor. Then we removed the lifting beams.

Some of the interior walls were missing, and the outside walls leaned out. We braced the outside walls and rebuilt the inside walls. Then we attached cables to the outside walls and pulled them back into place. The bay-window frames were badly damaged, and we rebuilt them, too. In the original building, few of the dimensions of the frames were exact or the angles correct. Thus, the re-built bays looked alike to the casual observer, but to the meticulous carpenter they were slightly different in both size and angle.

We continued to work outside and inside the depot through 2006 and 2007. For example, we continued yearly to replace the tarp over the roof. In the ten years, from 1997 to 2007, the roof deteriorated to the point that no one could walk on it. A borrowed bucket truck provided the only way to drape still another tarp on top of the declining roof.

In 2007, work on the depot halted. The Town of East Fishkill, in which the hamlet of Hopewell Junction is located, withdrew its funding. From 2007 to 2010, the best we could do was to replace the tarp every year and keep the incessant weeds from springing up around the building. By 2010, the depot deteriorated even more both outside and inside due to its exposure to the weather and the failing tarps. The Hopewell Junction Depot Restoration Corporation did not have enough money to repair the roof.

Dutchess County was in the early stages of planning a rail trail that would follow the rail bed of the bygone Dutchess County Railroad that ran from Poughkeepsie to Hopewell Junction and that obviously would pass by the only partially restored, mostly deteriorated depot. The situation looked very bleak not only for the depot but also for the few remaining volunteers who still wanted to restore it to its former dignity. Then, at this low point in our efforts and morale, I called Rich Taylor, the founder of the Hopewell Junction Depot Restoration Corporation.

Discovering a Plan: Richard Taylor

On the afternoon of October 12, 2010, I got a call from Bernie Rudberg. I could tell by the tone of his voice that he was in serious trouble. He told me he had just come from a meeting with Charlie Traver, then the commissioner of the Dutchess County Department of Public Works. Traver told Bernie he would have to come up with a plan to restore the depot in two days or the depot would be demolished.

Bernie told me there was machinery parked near the depot. I thought the machines were there to work on the Dutchess County rail trail and not on the depot. I told Bernie not to worry; nothing was going to happen to the depot. I said I would come up with a plan including funding, send the plan to the county, and set up a date to meet with Charlie Traver.

After Bernie hung up, I started to put a plan together showing that the work to restore the depot would be done within two years. My "Restoration Plan" outlined five phases of construction:

Phase 1: Complete all weatherproofing of the building by December 31, 2010.

Phase 2: Complete all exterior restoration of the building by July 2011.

Phase 3: Complete all interior restoration of the building to make ready for public assess by August 2012.

Phase 4: Set up interior with furnishings, artifacts, pictures, etc.; and

Phase 5: Complete exterior grounds and decking by June 2013 or earlier depending on funding.

Phase 6: Funds to complete all five phases will come from members' dues, donated materials, grants, and other funding efforts.

On that day, October 12, my dream of saving and restoring the depot was also restored after fourteen years of witnessing a steady decline in the condition of the depot and a steady decline in the efforts and interest of the volunteers to restore it. Work on the depot had gone slowly in those years, and money had been hard to come by. We had brought in some funds through donations and selling T-shirts sponsored by local businesses.

As time went on, from 1997 to 2007, the original Board of the Hopewell Depot Restoration Corporation (HDRC) started losing members. They left either out of a lack of interest or out of frustration. It had taken too long to work on the depot because of a lack of funds. I was not as deeply involved in the restoration as I had been at the beginning because of my construction business and my participation in Habitat for Humanity both in Dutchess County and around the United States.

Several days after Bernie's phone call, I met with Charlie [Traver]. The first part of my plan was to tear off the existing, badly burned, water damaged original roof system and replace it with a trussed rafter system. Once the Dutchess County engineer discovered this phase of my plan, he sent a letter to Bernie to have the work on the roof stopped, to have an outside engineer reorganize my complete five-phase "Restoration Plan," and to submit the revised plan to the county engineer before doing any more work on the depot.

I had a feeling this revision would take several weeks. Since I had promised Bernie I would have the depot open to the public within two years, I along with three other volunteers continued to work on the demolition of the original roof system and on straightening the outside walls. After receiving the new re-engineered plans six weeks later, I did not care for the design of the gable overhang, so I continued with my plan to keep the original gable design of the depot.

Realizing the Plan: Richard Taylor

We kept moving forward with our small crew working every Saturday and even Sundays. I wrote an article for the *Poughkeepsie Journal* seeking help. No one got back to me. We had been struggling with three snowstorms without a roof on the depot, and it was getting time to install the trusses. Since there were only four of us, I scheduled my friend and his cherry picker to help lift up the trusses on January 15, 2011, at 8 am.

That morning, as we five got started to work with the temperature at three degrees below zero, I noticed more and more trucks come into the depot parking lot. I knew then with the added twenty-five new volunteers we could install not only all the trusses but also all the plywood sheathing in one day. That day was the end of any more ice and snow in the depot. That day I knew we could restore the depot.

I was never worried about having enough money or volunteers to restore the depot. An anonymous local businessman donated funds to pay for the trusses and the plywood sheathing. Since I was skilled in construction and in working with volunteers, the restoration went along as planned. We worked every Saturday and started working on Wednesdays as well. That work schedule continues even today.

My second major plan was to restore and paint the exterior of the depot. This activity attracted even more volunteers and funding. We set up an incentive for volunteers and sponsors by having their names etched on plaques mounted on the outside walls of the depot.

In the fall of 2011, I appeared before the East Fishkill Town Board and explained to them how much a new roof for the depot was going to cost. I did not ask for money. After my presentation, the members of the board huddled. When they broke their huddle, they agreed to present to me on behalf of the Depot Restoration Corporation $11,000.00 and arranged to have Toll Brothers install the roof. The formal presentation of this arrangement was September 22.

During this time, Bernie Rudberg wrote two of his three books, *Hopewell Junction: A Railroader's Town* and *Twenty-Five Years on the ND&C: A History of the Newburgh, Dutchess, and Connecticut Railroad*. Both volumes were sold at the Depot and at speaking engagements he gave to historical societies and associations and to civic organizations. Bernie's efforts contributed to funding for the depot and made him a noted authority on the history of the several railroads in Dutchess County."

Double Heading

Bernard L. Rudberg's and Richard Taylor's joint extensive efforts complemented each other. The following railroad metaphor suggests the relationship of the twin specific acts of restoring both an obscurely recorded, scarcely recounted railroad history and an abandoned, dilapidated, ramshackle railroad station.

The reader most likely has seen two locomotives attached to the front of a train, one facing forward and the other facing backward, coupled together end-to-end. Railroaders call this assemblage "double heading." Rudberg's and Taylor's restorations were not separate but joined and united. As with double-headed locomotives, one restoration effort faced backward considering the historical past of the short-line railroads in Dutchess County, and the other restoration effort faced frontward considering the future vision of a reinstated, refurbished Hopewell Junction Depot.

As the double-heading locomotives work together in a mutual union to pull the train forward effectively and efficiently toward its destination, the two restoration efforts worked mutually. The restoration of the historical past discovered the obscurely recorded details of the railroad history;

reported those details; and applied them to the accurate restoration of the depot—and beyond to the building of the replica of Signal Station #196. Without this mutual work, the history of the short-line railroads of Dutchess County and the Hopewell Junction depot would have disintegrated. Instead, they exist simultaneously within books on shelves and without on Railroad Avenue in Hopewell Junction.

The Motivation and Dynamics of Volunteers

Rich Taylor and Charlie MacDonald

What motivated us to build an exact replica of the Signal Station #196 was the need for restrooms. The women who volunteered at the depot had to drive into Hopewell Junction to use a restroom. We had invited a group of senior citizens to tour the depot. After the group arrived and just before we began the tour, they asked to use the restrooms. We had none to offer. The incensed leader of the group said the tour was over before it began and escorted the seniors back on the bus, presumably in search of restrooms elsewhere. It was after that incident that we decided to build restrooms for future visitors as well as to build a replica of the Signal Station #196 to add to the restored depot.

We worked from several old, black-and-white photographs showing the Signal Station in the late nineteenth and early twentieth centuries. We also used plans Bernard Rudberg had collected from the files of the Newburgh, Dutchess, and Connecticut Railroad. We began construction in the fall of 2014, continued through the relatively dry and warm winter of 2015, and finished in the spring of 2015.

The original signal station did not have a foundation but just sat on the ground. We built a foundation for the restroom apparatus, a state-of-the-art, environmentally sound system. In the original signal station, the bottom floor was probably used for storage of signal equipment. In the replica signal station, the bottom floor is for the restrooms themselves. These restrooms are not only available to visitors of the depot but also to users of the Dutchess County rail trail that runs past the station. In both the original and the replica, the second floor is the signalmen's office. The original signal station had twenty signal levers. Two signal levers were donated to us, and those two are installed and in movable condition in the signalmen's office.

Our next big project is to build a pavilion twenty feet by forty feet to provide a place for depot and rail trail visitors to stop, rest, picnic, or enjoy a casual meeting place. We have the plans completed, but we need to get the proper insurance to protect not only the users of the pavilion but also the Depot Restoration Corporation.

Celeste Rudberg

I joined HDR (Hopewell Depot Restoration) in 1996 as a family member with my husband, Bernie. I have always been a lover of history. When I saw Rich's item in the paper that a group was forming to try to save the depot, I called it to Bernie's attention and suggested we get involved since we both loved history, and he loved the railroads.

The most I did, as I recall, was help clean up the area on the outside and paint pictures on the plywood covering the windows to let would-be vandals know that someone owned the building. I also attempted to sell T-shirts and to hand out brochures. The project I am most proud of was obtaining our IRS 501 (c) 3 designation. At a meeting in late 2010, one of our volunteers raised the question of whether we were a 501 (c) 3. Bernie, who was doubling as president and treasurer at the time, said our designation was a 501 (c) 7 instead. In addition, I have worked on fund-raising projects (which I am the least fond of) and acted as a tour guide.

Joe Sullivan

I joined in 2011 as a building volunteer after seeing folks working on the depot as I was coming back from a bike ride on the Dutchess County rail trail. A major part of the work had been completed. Cleaning and painting the exterior and finishing the interior were in process. I joined because I wanted to gain more construction experience and be a part of a historic restoration. I helped to complete working on the building restoration. For three years, I was the president of the organization.

Paul Stitch

I joined the Depot group in December 2011. The roof was completed, the exterior was painted, and much of the interior structural work was done. I was interested in the restoration project because historically Hopewell Junction originated as a railroad town, and the depot group was seeking to preserve and propagate its heritage.

Since I joined, I helped complete the interior restoration and all the work on the signal tower. My primary involvement has been in designing the museum, acting as a tour guide, publishing the newsletter, and curetting the collection. I created the various informational panels hanging on the wall of the depot waiting room that serves as a museum. I continue to curate the museum and publish the newsletter.

I also have established the structure of field trips for elementary and middle-school students. Hopewell Junction has been a community in transition for the past half century. By educating newcomers and current residents on the origins of the hamlet, the depot and its staff can nurture and perpetuate a sense of belonging. Properly cultivated, this education should translate into a desire to be of service on a local level.

Charlie MacDonald

I joined the Hopewell Depot Restoration Corporation probably in April 2112. I designed and built the diorama representing the history of the Junction in the 1920s. It is based on drawings and photos of the yard and the buildings surrounding it. The Junction changed constantly, according to the drawings and the photos. I am curious how the coal pocket worked. I think I have figured how the workers positioned the coal cars on the coal pit, released the coal into the pit, and conveyed the coal up to the pockets themselves.

Laura Wiegand

I started volunteering at the depot in October of 2011. I had retired and moved to Hopewell Junction. Rich, Maureen (Rich Taylor's wife), Bernie, and Celeste inspired the volunteers to keep working. I worked on the roof, under the building, on the ceiling, on the floor, and on the walls. Thank goodness for the skilled construction people!

After the depot building was restored, we had to assemble museum displays and a storage shed for tools and lumber. I helped out with grand openings, receptions, and traveling displays. One of the community outreach events is the East Fishkill Community Day. We started building parade floats in 2012. Charlie and I have been on the float committee for the last five years, and we've won first or second place awards every year!

Joyce and Dave Pfirman

David and I became members of the depot in the fall of 2015. Having recently retired, we were looking for a local organization with which we could both get involved. Since joining, I have been involved with the museum as a greeter and tour guide. I have taken on the scheduling of volunteers for the museum and handle membership. I have been part of the team that welcomes groups of school children to present the history of the depot.

We continue to look for new people in the community to support the depot through contributions. This enables us to operate the depot and expand the park surrounding the building as an attraction for the community. Through visiting the depot and other outreach functions throughout the year, we encourage new memberships.

Dave has been involved with the construction team and was part of the group that built the signal-tower replica. He became involved in the Board of Directors and is now president.

Linda Heitman

The beauty of the physical restoration was the first catalyst for me to join the Depot Restoration Cooperation. A call for volunteers in an article by Rich Taylor that appeared in the *Poughkeepsie Journal* in December 2017 sparked a desire to deepen my own knowledge of both local history in general and railroad history in particular. Lastly, a welcoming first meet with the Restoration volunteers made me want to be a part of this group.

Since joining, I have served as a greeter and tour guide for both regular station hours as well as special events (students and seniors), served on both the fundraising committee and as a director of our board, and submitted an application for museum charter status to the New York State Education Department that was granted in January 2018.

John Desmond

I joined the Hopewell Junction Depot Restoration Corporation the same day as Linda Heitman. I have conducted interviews with a former train engineer and a former fireman who drove trains by the depot, a former station agent who worked at the depot, a track-maintenance worker who often used the depot as headquarters, a long-time farm customer of the depot and residents of Hopewell Junction. These interviews create a living history of the depot.

I would like to see the depot acquire a caboose. Of all the cars included in a freight train today, the caboose is seldom if ever seen. Thus, to exhibit a caboose open to visitors would be an exceptional experience both for those who remember them and for those who have never seen one before.

The histories of the railroads that ran through Dutchess County, of the depot itself, and of the Hamlet of Hopewell Junction are complex. Mastering those histories has opened my eyes to the history of Dutchess County, a place I have lived in for thirty-six years, yet, it seems to me now, I had known little about.

Joe Sullivan approached me to ask if I would write the application for first a New York State historical site and second a national historic site. Both those goals have been accomplished as of March 2021.

Hopewell Junction Depot Museum

"The Board of Regents for and on behalf of the Education Department of the State of New York at their meeting of December 12, 2017, voted that a provisional charter valid for a term of five years is granted incorporating

[. . .] an educational cooperation under the cooperate name of Hopewell Depot Museum, located at Hopewell Junction, county of Dutchess, and state of New York."

Hopewell Junction Depot State and National Historic Site

The New York State Office of Parks, Recreation, and Historic Preservation certified that the Hopewell Junction depot in recognition of its significance in American history and culture as a historical resource was listed on the State Register of Historical Places on March 19, 2020.

The US Department of the Interior, National Parks Service, certified that the Hopewell Junction depot in recognition of its significance in American History and Culture as an architectural resource was listed on the National Register of Historical Places on February 24, 2021.

Retracing Charlotte Dodge's Footsteps Ninety-Nine Years Later

Because Charlotte Dodge is exceptionally detailed in her chronicle of a typical walk through the main streets of Hopewell Junction in 1923, it is simple for one to walk in her footsteps.

Next to what was once the Stevens house, there is neither an apple orchard nor the Red Onion Hotel and Bar. In place of the latter is a driveway. The driveway forks. The right fork leads to a storage center, and the left fork leads to a hardware store and lumber yard.

There are no tracks to cross; no watchman's shack to peer inside; and no watchman standing outside to caution a walker to stop, look, and listen if there is a train coming. Instead, there is a bridge to cross that arches high enough to make a walker forget there is even one single remaining track below it.

At the end of the bridge, on the right-hand side, there is a paved ramp that leads down to the paved rail trail that runs from Hopewell Junction south to the Connecticut state line, following the one remaining track first built by the NY&NERR in 1881.

The presence of the track reminds the walkers, runners, joggers, and cyclists who make their way along this rail trail that once a railroad ran along here from New Haven, Connecticut; through Danbury, Connecticut; up to Hopewell Junction; beyond to Poughkeepsie; and across the Poughkeepsie-Highland Railroad Bridge. Information plaques erected at the foot of the ramp and on the rail trail recite this information.

The walker may choose not to follow the rail trail but turn in the opposite direction to the north and under the bridge. There is no Turner's Hotel and Bar to avoid, no Kupiec's Lunch to consider entering, and no firehouse to visit. Hungry patrons of the rail trail may want to eat at the current bar and grill that occupies the space where Turner's was.

The walker follows the rail trail up to the restored Hopewell Junction depot, the replicated Signal Station #196, and the Bernard L. Rudberg Pavilion. Across from the depot sprawls a welding shop situated on land once occupied by the rail yard.

Unlike Charlotte Dodge, the walker may notice a lot of bustling around the depot caused not by passengers waiting for a train but by walkers, runners, joggers, and cyclists resting in the Bernard L. Rudberg Pavilion and refreshing in the restrooms of the replicated Signal Station #196, sponsored by the Hopewell Depot Museum. The rail trail continues north, passes the depot up to Poughkeepsie and the Walkway over the Hudson. This northern section is named the William R. Steinhaus Rail Trail

Inside the depot, there are no bathroom or tickets to inspect, as Charlotte and her friends did. However, on weekends, curious cyclists, joggers, runners, and walkers tour the inside of the Depot Museum and inspect its many rooms and displays.

The walker passes the depot and walks along Railroad Avenue but does not stop in the post office to pick up mail as the building is now a private residence. The walker crosses County Route 376 and comes up on Steven's Store, now a car and truck repair shop, and across the street the coal-and-feed store, now a ramshackle building. The walker stares into the empty space beyond this building to where the creamery and steam-engine-repair shop thrived and sees now an overgrown field used by the welding shop to park old trucks and store metal scrap.

Only the Hopewell Inn and the Burtis Hotel remain. The former is still a restaurant, while the latter is a private residence.

While crossing the one remaining track from Beacon to Hopewell Junction, the walker, like Charlotte Dodge, does not hear the whistle of an approaching train—or more likely—the very occasional horn of a

Metro-North Railroad pick-up truck riding the rails. Nothing else runs on the track,

Continuing, the walker notices the buildings that contained Grumbly's Store and Meat Market. These buildings are now private residences or occupied by small businesses. The blacksmith's shop and Tompkins's Store are gone.

At the intersection of routes 376 and 82, the walker does see a gas station, a market, and the private residence next to the market. The church hall is now an antique shop. Private residences and a funeral home are on the same side of the street as Charlotte Dodge's residence.

Charlotte Dodge's Hopewell Junction moved away from the railroads and Railroad Avenue. The businesses moved out of the rectangle that shaped Hopewell Junction and went west along Route 82 and Route 52 and south along Route 376.

The principal reason for the migration was the International Business Machine (IBM) plant built in 1963. It offered new jobs to the residents of East Fishkill and to computer engineers and businesspeople from elsewhere in Dutchess County and beyond. Farmlands were sold to developers who erected the plazas and built the several housing developments for mostly the employees of IBM to live. The IBM plant is gone now, too, but its large campus is occupied by several smaller businesses in an industrial park. Nonetheless, the hamlet that extends west along Route 82 and south along Route 376 is still called Hopewell Junction.

Younger residents born and raised in the hamlet and surrounding towns often wonder why the hamlet is called Hopewell Junction—until they happen upon Railroad Avenue, ride down this street, park in the rail-trail parking lots, and discover the restored depot sitting there.

Writing in 1969 in his book *A Short Haul to the Bay: A History of the Narragansett Pier Railroad*, James N. J. Henwood observes that "[i]n a day when even railroad giants find it necessary to merge and diversify, short line railroads are an anachronism. Most were built in an age when rail transportation represented the most modern and efficient kind available, and often they were designed to serve specific, limited purposes" (4).

Today, railroads are not the "most modern and efficient kind [of transportation] available," and automobiles and trucks are "designed to serve specific, limited purposes." Acquainting the younger residents of

Hopewell Junction and the surrounding towns with the local history of the Hopewell Junction depot is acquainting them with the history of the "specific, limited purposes" of their towns and with the history of a mode of transportation once "the most modern and efficient kind available"—150 years ago. The depot is a railroad relic that survived dilapidation and near destruction, and now, restored, it reminds its visitors of the vision, the ambition, the technology, the government permission, the legal framework, the initial finances, and the labor needed to build a railroad.

Appendix

Recent Photographs of the Restored Depot, the Replicated Signal Station, and the Newly Constructed Bernard Rudberg Pavilion

North Side of the Restored Hopewell Junction Depot Museum. Photograph by Richard Taylor from the Collection of Richard and Maureen Taylor, Courtesy of Richard and Maureen Taylor.

East Side of the Restored Hopewell Junction Depot Museum. Photograph by Richard Taylor from the Collection of Richard and Maureen Taylor, Courtesy of Richard and Maureen Taylor.

South Side of the Restored Hopewell Junction Depot Museum. Photograph by Richard Taylor from the Collection of Richard and Maureen Taylor, Courtesy of Richard and Maureen Taylor.

West Side of the Hopewell Junction Depot Museum. Photograph by Richard Taylor from the Collection of Richard and Maureen Taylor, Courtesy of Richard and Maureen Taylor.

West Waiting Room of the Hopewell Junction Depot Museum. Photograph by Richard Taylor from the Collection of Richard and Maureen Taylor, Courtesy of Richard and Maureen Taylor.

Station Agent's Office of the Hopewell Junction Depot Museum. Photograph by Richard Taylor from the Collection of Richard and Maureen Taylor, Courtesy of Richard and Maureen Taylor.

Telegrapher's Office of the Hopewell Junction Depot Museum. Photograph by Richard Taylor from the Collection of Richard and Maureen Taylor, Courtesy of Richard and Maureen Taylor.

East Waiting Room of the Hopewell Junction Depot Museum. Photograph by Richard Taylor from the Collection of Richard and Maureen Taylor, Courtesy of Richard and Maureen Taylor.

West Side of the Replica of Signal Station #196. Photograph by Richard Taylor from the Collection of Richard and Maureen Taylor, Courtesy of Richard and Maureen Taylor.

South Side of the Replica of Signal Station #196. Photograph by Richard Taylor from the Collection of Richard and Maureen Taylor, Courtesy of Richard and Maureen Taylor.

Bernard Rudberg Pavilion, Hopewell Junction Depot Museum. Photograph by Richard Taylor from the Collection of Richard and Maureen Taylor, Courtesy of Richard and Maureen Taylor.

Works Cited

Anthony, William N. *Hopewell Weekly News, The.* 5 Jan.–25 May 1899. Hopewell Junction, N.Y. 1899–1900. Print.
Beer Maps. 1867 and 1876. *Maps Available on Line 1800–1899.* Web. 5 May 2021.
Beneway, Jr. Howard. Personal Interview. 10 Feb. 2018.
Board of Railroad Commissioners of the State of New York. *Railroad Map of the State of New York 1894.* New York: G. W. & C. B. Colton & Co. 1894. Web. Library of Congress. https://lccn.loc.gov/98688529. 1 Jun. 2021.
Brown, James F. *Diary.* 26 Jul. 1849 and 20 Dec. 1849 Entries. MS. James F. Brown Papers. New York Heritage Digital Collection of James F. Brown diaries. https://cdm16694.contentdm.ocle.org/digital/collection/pl15052coll5/id/27565/.
Buckman, David Lear. *Old Steamboats on the Hudson River.* 1907. North Charleston, South Carolina: CreateSpace, 2021. Print.
Cochrane, Kent. *Steam Locomotive and Diesel Locomotive.* 1950. Photograph Bernard and Celeste Rudberg Collection.
Davies, Dr. Brian. "Before the Photocopier." *Ceredigion Archives.* N.p. n.d. Web. 15 Dec. 2020.
DeJoseph, Tom. Personal Interview. 16 Jun. 2017.
Di Gianfrancesco. *Materials for Ultra-Supercritical and Advanced Ultra-Supercritical Power Plants.* Cambridge, United Kingdom: Woodhead Publishing, 2017. Print.
Dodge, Charlotte. "Historic Hopewell." Hopewell Reformed Church. East Fishkill, N.Y. 17, March 2001.
Douglas, Frederick. *My Bondage and My Freedom.* New York: Miller, Orton, and Mulligan, 1855. *Railroads and the Making of Modern America.* A Digital History Project. n.d. Web. 2 Jul. 2021.
Dyni, Anne Quinby. *Niwot Colorado: Birth of a Railroad Town.* Charleston, S.C.: The History Press. 2011. Print.

"Excursion Trip over the Boston, Hartford, and Erie Railroad." *Poughkeepsie Eagle* reprinted in the *Fishkill Standard*. Fishkill, New York] 1870. Print.

Ferro, John. "Lincoln's last stop in Poughkeepsie: Sights 'never to be seen again.'" *Poughkeepsie Journal* 2 Apr. 2015, Updated ed.: *Poughkeepsiejournal.com/ story/* Web. News/local/central dutchess. 12 Feb. 2021.

Friedrichsen, Dieter. "The History of the Poughkeepsie and Eastern Railroad 1832–1937. Salt Point: n.p., 2015.

Gordon, Sarah H. *Passage to Union: How the Railroads Transformed American Life, 1829-1929*. London: Elephant Paperbacks, 1997. Print.

"Great Public Improvement, A." *Poughkeepsie Telegraph*. 9 Jan.1850. *Upper Landing History*. By George Lukacs. Web. 11 Mar. 2021.

Haight, Lyndon A. *Pine Plains and the Railroads*. Pine Plains, New York: Little Nine Partners Historical Society, 1976. Print.

"Harlem Railroad Opened." *The Journal and Poughkeepsie Eagle*. 6 Jan. 1849. Poughkeepsie, New York.

Harlow, Alvin F. *The Road of the Century*. New York: Creative Age Press, Inc. 1947. Print.

Haviland, Jim. "Lincoln's 'Ghost train' stopped in Poughkeepsie." Interview with Maura Shaw. *Poughkeepsie Journal*. [Poughkeepsie, New York] 27 Oct. 2014: B1. Print.

Henwood, James N. J. *A Short Haul to the Bay: A History of the Narragansett Pier Railroad*. Brattleboro, Vermont: The Stephen Green Press, 1969. Print.

Hiltzik, Michael. *Iron Empires: Robber Barons, Railroads, and the Making of Modern America*. New York: Houghton Mifflin Harcourt, 2020. Print.

Hyatt, E. Clarence. *History of the New York and Harlem Railroad*. N.p. n.p. 1898. Web. 9 Nov. 2020.

Jacobs, Harriet. *Incidents in the Life of a Slave Girl*. Massachusetts: n.p., 1861. *Railroads and the Making of Modern America*. A Digital History Project. n.d. Web. 2 Jul. 2021.

Jackson, Vern. Personal Interview. 24 Apr. 2018.

Kimball, Charles. "Telegraph Message to Van Buskirk." 11 Feb. 1884. In *The Newburgh, Dutchess, and Connecticut Railroad's Letter Books: 1879-1904*. Beacon Historical Society, Beacon, N.Y.

Kirkland, Edward Chase. *Men Cities and Transportation: A Study in New England History 1820-1900*. Vol. 2 Cambridge: Harvard University Press, 1948. Cited in Turner, Gregg M. *The New York and New England Railroad*. Conneaut Lake PA: Page Publishing, Inc, 2020.

Klein, Daniel B. and Gordon J. Fielding. "Private Toll Roads: Learning from the 19th Century." *Transportation Quarterly* 46, no. 3 (July 1992: 321–341. University of California Transportation Center. Berkeley, California: 1992. Web. Jun. 2021.

Levinson, Nancy Smiler. *She's Been Working on the Railroad*. New York: Lodestar Books, 1997. Print.

Lubar, Steven. "Promoting the Hudson River Railroad." *Railroad History*, Nu. 157 Autumn 1987: 55–63, Railroad & Locomotive Historical Society, www.jstor.org/stable/43523363.

Lund, David. Telephone Interview. 30 Dec. 2021.

Mabee, Carleton. *Listen to the Whistle*. Fleischmanns, N.Y.: Purple Mountain Press, 1995. Print.

McCue, Robert. "The End of the Newburgh Branch of the Erie Railroad." Telephone Interview. 29 Apr. 2021,

McCue, Robert. *Erie Railroad's Newburgh Branch*. Charleston, S.C.: Arcadia Publishing, 2014. Print.

McCue, Robert. *Erie Railroad Volume Three:" Ski Trains, Trackcars, and Trails."* Middletown, Del.: n.p. 28, Jun. 2021. 42–43.

Mc Dermott, William P. *Dutchess County Railroads*. Clinton, N.Y: Town of Clinton Historical Society, 1996. Print.

McEntee, Austen. *Hopewell Junction Depot after the Fire*." 1986, Private Collection of J. W. Swanberg.

McLachlan, Pete. Personal Interview. 9 Jun. 2017.

McLaughlin, D. W. "Poughkeepsie Gateway." *The Railroad and Locomotive Historical Society Bulletin*. No. 119 (Oct. 1968): 6–33. Print.

Majewski, John, Christopher Baer, and Daniel B. Klein. *Market and Community in Antebellum America: The Plank Roads of New York*. Working Paper No. 47. 1991. University of California Transportation Center, University of California at Berkeley. Web. scholarship.org. 12 Feb. 2021.

Mills, Malcolm J. *East Fishkill*. Charleston, S.C.: Arcadia Publishing, 2006. Print.

"Mortgage to John Crosby Brown, Esq., Trustee." Dutchess and Columbia Railroad Company. January 1, 1868. Web. 19 Nov. 2020.

Moseman, Barbara. Personal Interview. 1 Jul. 2018.

Moseman, James. Personal Interview. 2 Jul. 2018.

Mott, Harold. *Between the Ocean and the Lakes: The Story of Erie*. New York: Collins, 1899.

The Newburgh, Dutchess, and Connecticut Railroad's Letter Books: 1879–1904. Beacon Historical Society, Beacon, N.Y.

Osterberg, Mathew. *The Delaware and Hudson Canal and the Gravity Railroad*. Mount Pleasant, S.C.: Arcadia Publishing, 2002. Print.

"Overview: Mining Anthracite." *Stories from PA History*. ExplorePAHistory.com n.d. Web. 18 Jun. 2021.

Powell, H. Benjamin. "The Pennsylvania Anthracite Industry: 1769–1976." *Pennsylvania History: A Journal of Mid-Atlantic Studies* 47, no. 1, Pennsylvania State University Press. Jan. 1980, 3–28.

"Road Opened." *The Journal and Poughkeepsie Eagle.* 5 Jan. 1849. Poughkeepsie, New York.

Rubin, Julius. "Canal or Railroad? Imitation and Innovation in Response to the Erie Canal in Philadelphia, Baltimore and Boston." *Transactions of the American Philosophical Society.* New Series 51, Part 7 (1961): 6. Print.

Rudberg, Bernard L. *Hopewell Depot: Railroad Years and Restoration 1873–2013.* Hopewell Junction, N.Y.: Hopewell Junction Restoration Corp., 2013. Print.

Rudberg, Bernard L. *The Newburgh, Dutchess, and Connecticut Railroad's Letter Books at the Beacon Historical Society, Beacon, N.Y.* 2002.

Smith, James H. "Early Transportation in Dutchess County—Part 3: Chapter XI." *History of Dutchess County, New York.* New York: D. Mason and Co., 1882. Print.

Stewart, Inglis. *The Dutchess and Columbia R.R. and Its Associates.* N.p. n.p. n.d.

Swanberg, Jack. Telephone Interview. 10 Apr. 2017.

Taylor, Richard. Interview by John Desmond. "We Can Still Hear the Whistle Blowin.'" *The Speed Witch* 7, no. 1, 2018: 11–16. Print.

Tamaney, Mary. "Giant Social Gathering of 1850." *Times Hudson Valley.* timeshudsonvalley.com. 23 Apr. 2020. Web. 15 Feb. 2021.

Turner, Gregg M. *The New York and New England Railroad.* Conneaut Lake, PA: Page Publishing, Inc., 2020.

Vanderbilt, Cornelius. "I'll Tell You." *New York Herald* September 19, 1873. Print. In Hiltzik, Michael. *Iron Empires: Robber Barons, Railroads, and the Making of Modern America.* New York: Houghton Mifflin Harcourt, 2020. Print.

Williams, David. Personal Interview. 18 Aug. 2021.

Wilson, Jeff. *Milk Trains and Traffic.* Waukesha, Wisc.: Kalmbach Media, 2019. Print.

Wolman, Christian. *The Great Railroad Revolution.* 2012. New York: Public Affairs, 2013. Print.

Index

accounts
  driving trains through Hopewell Junction, 105-7
  firing trains through Hopewell Junction, 107-9
  last Poughkeepsie-to-Hopewell Junction run, 121-22
  living in Hopewell Junction, 91-101
Anthony, William H., 80
anthracite (coal), mining for, 13-15
anthracite coal, 30-31
  alternative train for, 63-65
  coal rush, 13-15
  transporting, 46-48

Baldwin Locomotive Works, 43
Beneway, Howard, Jr., 112-15, 120-21
Blacks, employing, 37
block, 110
boardroom mergers, 79-80, 117-19
Book of Rules, 110-11
Boston, Hartford, and Erie Railroad (BH&ERR), 18-19, 25, 28, 56, 69-70
  inaugural run of, 19-21
bridges, 44-46. *See also* xxx
Brown, George H., 17-19, 30, 61, 65

Brown, Hunter G., 60
Brown, James F., 10
Brown, John Crosby, 28
Bryant, C. W., 60
buildings, moving, 84-86

can cars, 49
Central New England and Western Railroad (CNE&WRR), 79
Central New England Railroad (CNERR), 32
  end of ND&CRR, 86-87
  relocating Hopewell Depot, 83-86
charcoal, 59-60, 128
Chevalier, C. N., 52
Clarkson University Hudson River Extension, 39
Clove Branch Railroad (CBRR), 30, 42-43, 59-63
Columbia County, 64
Connecticut and Western Railroad (C&WRR), 18-19
Connecticut General Assembly, 6
Conrail, 118-19
  last Poughkeepsie-to-Hopewell Junction run, 121-22
consolidation locomotive, 77-78

153

convergence, 66–67
Cooper, Elizabeth, 106, 109–12, 112
Cornell Steamboat Company, 63–65
Cornell, Thomas, 63–65

Danbury Railroad Museum, 119
Danbury, Connecticut, 25
Davies, Brian, 31
DeJoseph, Thomas, 109–12
Delaware and Hudson Canal, 46
Delaware and Hudson River, 16
depot. *See* Hopewell Junction
Desmond, John, 137
diesels, phasing in, 103–5
Dodge, Charlotte, retracting footsteps of, 138–41
Douglass, Frederick, 10
Dutch Reformed Church, 21
Dutchess and Columbia Railroad (D&CRR), 16, 17–19
　ending of, 26–28
　New Hopewell depot, 25–26
Dutchess County Ralroad (DCRR), 72, 74–76
　boardroom mergers, 78–79
　issuing charter to, 6
　and P&ERR, 53
　relocating Hopewell Depot, 83–86
Dutchess County, New York
　coal in, 46–48
Dutchess County, 119
Dutchess County Railroad Company (DCRR), 6
Dutchess County, New York, ND&CRR, 1–2, 11, 35–37, 47
　Denning's Point, 18–19
　on maps, 39–40
　NY&HRR in, 7–9
　state of economy, 11–13

Dyni, Anne Quinby, 23

East Fishkill, 1
East Fishkill Community Day, 136
East Tennessee and Virginia Railroad (ET&VRR), 30
economy, 11–13
Edward, Alfred, 96–97
equipment, buying/selling, 40–43
Erie Canal, 16
Erie Railroad (ERR), 15–16, 47
　first Newburgh Branch, 6–7
eyewitnesses. *See* accounts

farms, 8
ferry, 6, 18, 36–39, 47, 50, 61, 71–72, 76, 86
Financial Panic of 1873, 26–28
firemen, 8, 19, 37, 51, 100, 105–9, 119–20, 127, 137
Fish Landing, ND&CRR, 37–40
Fishkill Landing, 6, 10, 47, 52
　and NY&NERR, 69–71
Fishkill Methodist Sunday School, 60
Fishkill Standard, 19–20, 55
fog, 51
Friedrichsen, Dieter, 58

"Giant Social Gathering of 1850," 15–16
gondolas, 62
Gordon, Sarah H., 27
Great Blizzard, 48
Great Depression. *See* Financial Panic of 1873
Great Railroad Revolution, The (Wolmar), 5–6, 125

Haight, Lyndon A., 65

Hampshire and Hamden Railroad (H&HRR), 30
Harlem Valley Railroad, 56
Hartford, Providence, and Fishkill Railroad (HP&FRR)
 bankruptcy of, 6–7
Heitman, Linda, 136
Henry, John, 9
Henwood, James N., 140
Highland-Poughkeepsie Bridge, 106
Hiltzik, Michael, 8–9
History of the New York and Harlem Railroad (Hyatt), 8
Hopewell Depot Restoration (HDRC), 127–29, 136
Hopewell Junction, 1, 19–21
 abandoned tracks, 87–90
 abandoning, 122–24
 accounts of living in, 91–101
 after rails reaching, 17–33
 birth of, 69–78
 boardroom mergers, 79–80
 changes to, 79–90
 depot station agents, 109–12
 development/expansion of, 80–83
 diesel locomotives at, 103–5
 Dutchess County Railroad, 74–76
 first settlement, 22, 100
 last revenue at, 121–22
 moving Dutchess Junction, 86–87
 name, 25
 NY&NERR reaching, 69–71
 and Poughkeepsie-Highland Bridge, 71–73
 railroad contentions in, 76–78
 rails departing, 117–24
 before rails reaching, 5–16
 relocating depot, 83–86
 restoring depot, 125–42

 second settlement, 20, 25, 37–38, 59, 69–70
Hopewell Weekly News, The, 80–83
Hopewell, settlements named, 21–25
Hudson Highlands State Park, 39
Hudson River, 6
Hudson River Railroad (HRRR), 9–11
Hyatt, E. Carence, 8

ice, 48–49
International Business Machine (IBM), 140
Iron Empires (Hiltzik), 8–9
iron ore, 12, 30, 42–43, 56, 59–60, 62, 74, 78

Jackson, Vern, 97–99
Jacobs, Harriett, 10, 11
James, Evert, 96–97
Journal and Poughkeepsie Eagle, 7, 9
Judson, Roswell S., 19, 30
junction, term, 25

Kimball, Charles L., 32–33, 35–37, 62, 76

Lackawaxen River, 14
Lawry, James, 32–33
Letter Books of the Newburgh, Dutchess, and Connecticut Railroad, The, 31–33
 bad weather, 50–52
 bridges, 44–46
 buying/selling equipment, 40–43
 Dutchess Junction, 35–37
 Fishkill Landing, 37–40
 transporting coal, 46–48
 transporting milk, 48–50
Levinson, Nancy Smiler, 21

Index | 155

Lincoln, Abraham, 11
Lubar, Steven, 5
Lund, David, 96–97

Mabee, Carleton, 71–73, 118–21
MacDonald, Charlie, 133–35
Majewski, John, 12–13
Maybrook Line, 85, 105
Maybrook Rail Yard, 117
McCue, Robert, 15
McDermott, William, 17, 56, 57
McLachlan, Peter, 105–7
McLaughlin, D. W., 27
McLeod, Angus, 79
Metro-North, 119
Metro-North Beacon, 39
milk car, 48–50
milk train, 48–50
Milk Trains and Traffic (Wilson), 48
milk, transporting, 48–50
Miller, E. I., 61
Morgan, J. Pierpont, 80
Moseman, Barbara/James, 99–101
My Bondage and My Freedom (Douglass), 10

New England Railroad (NERR), 80
New Haven Railroad, 108
New Haven, Connecticut, 105
New Paltz, 11
New York and Harlem Railroad (NY&HRR), 7–11, 19, 32, 50, 70–71
New York and Massachusetts Railway (NY&MRR), 57, 66–67
New York and New England Railroad (NY&NERR), 25, 69–71
  end of ND&CRR, 86–87
  and Fishkill Landing, 37–40
  railroad contentions, 76–78
  relocating Hopewell Depot, 83–86
New York Central and Hudson Railroad (NYC&HRR), 25, 32, 36–37, 39, 49–50
New York Central and Hudson River Railroad (NYC&RR), 35
New York Central Railroad (NYCRR), 62
New York Commercial Advertiser, 7
New York State Board of Railroad Commissioners, 60
New York State Park, 73
New York Times, 14
New York, Boston, and Montreal Railroad (NYB&MRR), 65–66
New York, Boston, and Northern Railroad (NYB&NRR), 65–66
New York, New Haven, and Hartford Railroad (NYNH&HRR), 57
  end of ND&CRR, 86–87
Newburgh, 16
Newburgh Branch, 47
Newburgh, Dutchess and Connecticut Railroad (ND&CRR)
  bad weather, 50–52
  beginning of, 28–31
  bridges, 44–46
  buying/selling equipment, 40–43
  Dutchess Junction, 35–37
  end of, 86–87
  Fishkill Landing, 37–40
  Letter Books, 31–33
  milk transportation, 48–50
  operational subjects of, 35–52
  railroad contentions, 76–78

rivals of, 53–68
transporting coal, 46–48
Newburgh, Dutchess, and Columbia Railroad (ND&CRR), 25, 88
Niwot Colorado: Birth of a Railroad Town (Dyni), 23

Passage to Union: How the Railroads Transformed American Life, 27
pasteurization, 48–49
Pauling Mountain, 104
paved roads, 87–90
Pelton, George, 57
Penn Central Railroad (PCRR), 117–20
Penn Coal Company, 15
Pennsylvania Railroad (PRR), 46, 117
Pennsylvania, coal rush in, 13–15
Pfirman, Joyce/Dave, 136
Philadelphia and Reading Railroad (P&RRR), 79
Philadelphia, Redding, and New England Railroad Company (PR&NERRC), 79
Phoenix Bridge Company, 45
Platt, Edmund, 53
Platt, Isaac, 54
Plum Point. *See* Dutchess Junction
Poughkeepsie, 11
Poughkeepsie and Eastern Railroad (P&ERR)
  family railroads, 65
  funding, 64
  labor dispute, 58
  as ND&CRR rival, 53–56
Poughkeepsie and Eastern Railroad Company (P&ERR), 57
Poughkeepsie and Eastern Railroad Company (P&ERRC), 62

Poughkeepsie and South Eastern Railroad (P&SERR), 74
Poughkeepsie Baptist Church, 61
Poughkeepsie Daily Eagle, 54
Poughkeepsie Eagle, 19–21, 25, 72–73
Poughkeepsie Journal, 105, 127, 131, 136
Poughkeepsie Locomotive Engine Company, 6
Poughkeepsie-Highland Bridge, 71–73, 74, 80, 86
  abandoning depot, 122–24
  burning of, 119–21
Poughkeepsie, Hartford, and Boston Railroad (PH&BRR), 57
"Promoting the Hudson River Railroad," 5

railroad line, 2–4
  birth of Hopewell Junction, 69–90
  failures, 6–7
  and paved-road revolution, 87–90
  purpose for building, 5–6
  rivalries, 53–68
  short-haul operating procedures, 35–52
  success of, 7–11
  working rails, 103–15
rails, working
  phasing in diesels, 103–5
  phasing out steam, 103–5
Ralph, J., 40
refrigerator cars, 50
Restoration Plan, Hopewell Junction Depot, 129–31
restoration, Hopewell Junction, 125
  depot museum, 137–38
  discovering Restoration Plan, 129–31

restoration, Hopewell Junction *(continued)*
  double heading, 132–33
  first effort, 127–29
  first glance, 126–27
  national historic site, 138
  realizing plan, 131–32
  retracting Dodge footsteps, 138–41
  volunteer motivation/dynamics, 133–37
revenue, 18, 28, 30, 49, 56–57, 59–62, 64, 81, 121
Rhinebeck and Connecticut Railroad (R&CRR), 63–65
rivals, ND&CRR
  Clove Branch Railroad, 59–63
  converging parallel lines, 66–67
  New York, Boston, and Montreal Railroad (NYB&MRR), 65–66
  old operations under new names, 57–58
  Poughkeepsie and Eastern Railroad (P&ERR), 53–56
  Rhinebeck and Connecticut Railroad, 63–65
road maps, 63
Rudberg, Bernard T., 127–29
Rudberg, Bernie, 132–33
Rudberg, Celeste, 134

Saunter, Charlotte Dodge, 91–96
Schultze, John L., 42, 76
Selkirk Rail Yard, 117
Selkirk-Castleton Bridge, 117–19
semaphore, 84
She's Been Working on the Railroad (Levinson), 21
short-haul railroad, operating procedures of

bad weather, 50–52
bridges, 44–46
buying/selling equipment, 40–43
Dutchess Junction, 35–37
Fishkill Landing, 37–40
milk transportation, 48–50
transporting coal, 46–48
Signal Station #196, 84, 89, 133, 139
Southern Dutchess News, 127
Spaight, John W., 55
State of New York, 9
Steam Locomotive #3558, 104–5
steam, phasing out, 103–5
Stitch, Paul, 135
Sullivan, Joe, 134
Swanberg, Jack, 107–9

Tamaney, Mary, 15–16
Taylor, Richard, 126–27, 129–31, 131–34
telegraph-telephone office, 51
Tioronda Bridge, 36, 44–46
traffic, 38–39, 45, 48–49, 59–61, 64, 70, 72, 74, 77, 84–86, 89, 96, 118
train orders, 110
trains, 7–8
  driving, 105–7
  firing, 107–9
  working on rails, 112–15
transportation, 12–13

Vanderbilt, Cornelius, 9, 27, 79
volunteers, motivation/dynamics of, 133–37

Washington, locomotive, 40–43
weather, coping with, 49, 50–52
Wicopee Junction, 36
Wiegand, Laura, 135–36

William T. Hart, ferry, 38, 48
Williams, Dave, 121–22
Wilson, Jeff, 48

wind, 51
Wolmar, Christian, 5–6, 58, 103, 125
women, employing, 21

www.ingramcontent.com/pod-product-compliance
Lightning Source LLC
Chambersburg PA
CBHW032026230426
43671CB00005B/218